五筆破分字

# CHINESE PAINTING

Third American Edition
published in the United States of America in 1967 by
UNIVERSE BOOKS, Inc.
381 Park avenue South
New York, N.Y. 10016

*Library of Congress Catalog Card Number 58-11096*

**PRINTED IN FRANCE**

PETER C. SWANN

# CHINESE PAINTING

UNIVERSE BOOKS, INC.--NEW YORK

# Introduction

THE aims of this book must of necessity be modest. It is obviously impossible, in such an introductory work, to treat fully an art produced by an unbroken tradition of two thousand years. One can only outline its history, give some essentials of its technique, discuss some of the fundamental ideas on which it is based and reproduce in colour a few of the finest paintings which have survived in Chinese and European collections. Its greatest possible success would be to stimulate the reader to seek more knowledge of a vast and fascinating field which we have only just begun to explore in depth.

The Chinese consider painting to be their only real art. The rest, for all their perfection, they think of as crafts. Why is it then that what the Chinese consider the finest flower of their culture is so little known in the West? For at least four centuries we have known and admired their porcelain and many other Chinese craft products brought to the west through extensive trade contacts. A Chinese vase takes its place in our homes as naturally as a Louis XVIth settee or a Sheraton chair. The West has gained a very one-sided idea of Chinese painting from the decorative products of craftsmen which came to Europe with the porcelain. Our first halting steps in the discovery of true Chinese painting were taken in this century.

Until comparatively recent times the technique and spirit of all but the most decorative Chinese painting were too strange for even the most informed western connoisseur to appreciate. The welcome which French painters gave to Japanese prints towards the end of the 19th century prepared the public for a revelation of something new in eastern painting. But the Chinese have guarded their real masterpieces jealously. Unlike porcelain, the finest paintings were never readily available for export. Chinese collectors have paid for their own treasures prices as high as those which great paintings command in the west. Thus, even after some fifty years of study this art of China remains comparatively unknown. Western private collectors, who are the life blood of our art studies, have hesitated to venture into the field. Whereas they will pay many thousands of pounds for a bronze or a fine example of a rare ceramic type, they are unwilling to pay as many hundreds for a Chinese landscape by a great master. The only exceptions to this rule are less than half a dozen private collectors and a few museums, notably in America. The absence of the private collector is the most serious for as Friedlander said "...if one enquires by whom and in what manner our knowledge has been enriched, one usually comes upon the lover of art who, independent of predecessors, has naively faced the works of art. Everyone must here start from scratch and be able to forget what he has read."

However lamentable this lack of appreciation may seem, it is not so strange when we reflect that even today the history and manifold achievements of Chinese civilisation find no place in the curriculums of our schools.

On the other hand, the historian and specialist must be prepared to admit that his knowledge of Chinese painting still rests on very unsteady foundations. Though the Chinese have written on painting *in extenso* from the 6th century onwards, nothing comparable to western critical studies developed in China. Western scholars, applying critical methods, have taken up the task with enthusiasm but still few monographs on individual painters exist. Only in the last two years has the greatest expert on Chinese painting, Professor Sirén of Sweden, dared to divide the existing ancient Chinese paintings into what he considers true and later copies. The task is fraught with difficulties.

The Chinese, until recently, have been the greatest lovers of tradition. The highest praise a painter can win is to be told that his work is indistinguishable from that of his master or from that of a master who lived centuries before him. The Chinese, while admiring a man's originality, demand first and foremost that he display this reverence for past achievements. Many a biography in Chinese will contain the admiring words, "His work could not be distinguished from that of such-and-such a master of the past." However, fortunately for the development of the art, it will frequently end with the phrase " Later in life he formed his own school." Copies abound. Some are not intended to deceive, for the painter will frankly state that he is copying an old master. Real forgeries are equally common and, so close has been the study of old masters that, in the present state of our knowledge, it is often difficult to distinguish the two. Studios exist for the reproduction of old masterpieces and they employ first class artists. A story is told of an eminent dealer who bought a number of outstanding paintings and left them in China to be packed and forwarded to him. He received a set of brilliant copies. From early times, signatures were copied and

8

seals forged. Unscrupulous keepers of collections, especially of Imperial collections, who were themselves lovers of the art, often substituted copies for originals. We are in truth only at the beginning of our studies. Thus this book will contain a number of paintings of which it is only possible to say "attributed to" a certain painter. But a number of these old paintings "attributed to" a famous artist are often outstanding works of art in themselves.

The westerner, looking at Chinese painting for this first time, must become accustomed to some unfamiliar aspects. He will find no oil painting. Scientific perspective, the study of which has so engrossed the west, has never interested the Chinese. They have solved the problem of representing what they call "the far and the near" in their own original manner. This, as we shall see, has enabled them to develop a unique form of landscape painting. Again, except for a relatively obscure genre of erotic painting, the study of the human form plays no part in the training of a Chinese painter. Chinese artists never felt that "only knowledge of the nude made the appearance of the clothed figure comprehensible." One can put this in another way by saying that man's position in the universe as envisaged by the Chinese is of less importance than in the west. Neither does the Chinese painter work directly from nature with his canvas before him adding a touch here, emphasing a shadow or a line there, mixing and changing his colours from a comprehensive palette. Nevertheless, the Chinese artist studies nature just as closely and perhaps associates himself even more intimately with it than his western counterpart. He may spend years of his life travelling to see the beauty spots of his land. But he produces his work of art in the stillness of a studio and generally only after long contemplation of what he has seen. A landscape in particular can be called the synthesis of his experiences in nature. It may be executed quite quickly with a few splashes and lines, it may be slowly built up from tiny brushstrokes. The materials he uses allow of few alterations. The artist's ideas must be clear, his technique sure and his execution spontaneous. These basic requirements ensure that a Chinese painting is the immediate expression of a man's personality.

Painting in colours has always been practised in China. It has much in common with our own water colours and examples are included in this book. But the greatest achievements of Chinese painting have been in monochrome. The appreciation of the possibilities of ink in all its shades on paper or silk was the great discovery of the Chinese. The ink the Chinese painter uses is a mixture of soot and glue pressed into sticks and dried. The artist puts a few drops of water on his ink-stone, rubs the stick in the water and in a few seconds has his complete palette. The brush he uses is a simple length of bamboo into which are fixed the hairs of various animals. Over the centuries the Chinese have developed what is basically no more than an ancient writing implement into the most sensitive instrument available to any painter. It reflects immediately every movement of the body. It must be wielded from the shoulder and elbow and not from the wrist. It can produce a line of any thickness and reveals completely the personality of the artist. "The brushstroke is the man." It is worth while pointing out a technical difference between western and far eastern painting brushes. In the western brush, the belly is near the tip and easily falls onto the canvas while in the far eastern brush it is near the root and always under control. Only years of practice can produce the control of body and discipline of mind which are needed to master it.

This expertise comes in the first place from calligraphy. We shall have very little space here to discuss the close relationship of calligraphy to painting. The former is considered an art in itself and valued as highly. A fine example of calligraphy mounted as a scroll will receive as much appreciation as a painting. The same brush and ink are used for both. If a Chinese has mastered the writing of the thousands of characters which make up the vocabulary of an educated man he has all the basic technique necessary for painting. The characters have their own subtleties of line and form and the rules for composing them are very strict. A piece of calligraphy is as revealing of its author's spirit as a painting. Often it forms an important part of a composition, for it may be a poem by the artist himself intended to increase the mood of the work. It may equally be a few lines of appreciation or authentification by a friend or a later connoisseur. More often than not in later art it addes to the beauty of a work by providing an added technical or emotional dimension. Sherman Lee made a useful analogy when he said "To the Chinese, the value-judgement of a picture rests primarily on its brushwork as related to and derived from calligraphy. The nearest we Westerners can get to the essence of what a Chinese sees in Chinese painting is our concept of *touch*.[1]" The brushstroke is the most important single factor in Chinese painting. For the Chinese the picture itself is not intended primarily as a wall decoration, and because the frame, simple or ornate, does not exist, the painting is never cut off from its surroundings. In every way it partakes closely of the world around it. It can be rolled up and stored away to be brought out only when friends deemed worthy of appreciating it are gathered together. It may sometimes be shown| for a few days, according to the season or to the occasion for which its owner considers it suited. It is like a book—to be read and enjoyed when the occasion demands.

The two principle forms are the vertical hanging scroll *Shou-chüan* (or *kakemono* to give it its more familiar Japanese name) and hand-scrolls *chou* (*makimono* in Japanese). *Makimono* are scrolls unrolled from right to left, section by section. They lead the spectator through an ever-changing landscape or from scene to scene. In their landscape manifestation they add a time element to painting which is unique to the Far East. We shall return to this subject later. The vertical hanging scrolls are essentially to be "read" from top to bottom.

Almost all subjects, religious and secular, with the exception of the nude, are found in Chinese painting. But it is in landscape that it excells. The Chinese discovered the art of pure landscape many centuries before the west. This is credited to Wang Wei (A.D. 699-759, see p. 48) and from his time onwards the beauty of landscape has never ceased to fascinate the Chinese painter. The expression of its infinite variety has been his permanent quest. He may be overwhelmed by its grandeur or dazzled by its soft beauty ; he may be amused by its humour. He may see it from far off as a vast panorama or he may be on intimate terms with a small part of it. He may humbly introduce himself into it but seldom, as in the west, does he presume to be its master. It remains an inexhaustible source of mystery. He approaches it with great respect.

This book is intended for the uninitiated. It includes no flights of literary fancy or philosophical speculation. It discusses Chinese painting in a straight-forward historical manner from its beginnings in the centuries immediately preceeding our era. With these we must begin.

# BEGINNINGS
## of
# CHINESE PAINTING

How little we know of the beginnings of any nation's art! One might expect that a civilisation, like the Chinese with an unbroken history of some three thousand five hundred years, might provide more opportunity to write of the birth of its pictorial art than others. But the great antiquity and fragility of the materials of Chinese painting make even its origins difficult to trace with any certainty. China has suffered its periods of destruction. Temples have been devastated during religious persecutions and vast collections, especially those of Emperors, have been put to the torch. Much of the most precious work has disappeared for ever. However, there can be no doubt that the origins of Chinese painting are indeed very early.

The skill with which neolithic pots of the third millenium B.C. are decorated, is worth comment. The vivid designs on these vessels owe their effect to most accomplished brushwork. Also bronze colour containers have been discovered which date from about 1000 B.C., and certainly some form of true painting, probably mural, was practised in these early times.

During the period of the great Chinese bronzes (*ca.* 1300 B.C.-A.D. 200), the decoration of vessels generally took highly conventionalised and generally zoomorphic forms which were worked out in geometric terms and cast on the bronzes with unsurpassed skill. The involved symbolism of these designs, in spite of their imaginative power, are the very antithesis of the fluid line of painting—especially of Chinese painting—as we know it, and it is possible that the strict canons of decorative art prevented the Chinese from developing an art of painting to match that of the bronzes.

It was towards the middle of the first millenium B.C. that the Chinese began to develop the naturalistic approach to art which painting was eminently suited to express.

Literary works from pre-Han times contain intriguing references to actual paintings which have not survived. They also provide evidence of an appreciation of nature which is significant for the development of landscape painting. In the *Book of Songs*, which includes material from the 8th to the 6th century B.C., we find such charming lines as :

*Jagged are the rocks*
*Oh how high!*
*These hills and rivers go on and on.*
*It seems as though they would never end.*[2]

Even in such an early, unaffected poem we find two features which inspired two thousand years of Chinese painting—the dominating impressiveness of rocks and the broad continuity of rivers and hills.

Some centuries later, by the time of the poet Ch'ü Yüan (traditional dates 345-290 B.C.) one reads the melancholy but sensitive lines :

*Amid the deep wood, there in the twilight gloom*
*Are the haunts where the monkeys live.*
*The mountains' awful height screens the noonday sun,*
*And below is dark and dim with perpetual rain.*[3]

The feelings inspired by nature are here imbued with a deeper emotional content. This is significant for Ch'ü Yüan came from the south of China where the country is richer and the landscape with its rivers and mountains more atmospheric. As Chinese civilisation spread to the south of the country this southern strain increasingly influenced the sensibilities of the nation and enriched its art.

Technical as well as intellectual developments influence the emergence of an art. The origins of Chinese painting are necessarily connected with the invention of the brush. According to legend, it was invented by a certain Shih Huang who is reputed to have lived 2697—2597 B.C., but such cultural heroes credited with important inventions abound in Chinese mythology as they do in those of other peoples. The earliest actual brush discovered by archaeologists comes from Hui Hsien and probably dates to about the 4th century B.C. The birds, animals and geometric designs painted on lacquer objects that belong to this time were certainly painted with the brush.

For some centuries prior to the Christian era, we can only trace the first efforts of the Chinese to paint from craftworks like lacquer and bronze. For example, the reliefs on bronze vessels cast about 4th-3rd centuries B.C. (Pl. 15) give some indication of the ideas which stimulated them. Interspersed with the formalised decorations familiar from centuries of bronze casting are bands containing vivid hunting scenes. Some of the figures wear masks and suggest

14

# THE
# HAN DYNASTY
## 206 B.C. - 220 A.D.

THE first empire which a great civilisation creates leaves an indelible mark for better or worse on its subsequent history. The more successful the empire, the more lasting is its influence. For the Chinese, the Han Dynasty (206 B.C.-A.D. 220) was this great formative period. During the four hundred years of the Han many of the features which distinguish modern Chinese civilisation were firmly established.

China was united for the first time in 221 B.C. by a ruthless dictator Ch'in Shih Huang Ti. His dynasty did not survive him, but the unity which he imposed on the country lasted for the following four hundred years of his Han successors and gave China a conviction of the properness and inevitability of unity which it never forgot.

Under the Han, Chinese arms were carried into central Asia, Manchuria and Korea. Constant battles with the Hsiung-nu nomads pressing down from the north preserved the military vigour of the age. Chinese travellers reached as far as the Caspian sea and the silk trade across Asia resulted in the first indirect contacts with the Roman Empire. A civil service was created to rule this vast empire and appointment to it was by examination. Theoretically, the highest office in the state was open to the lowest born—a remarkable concept which has always inspired the Chinese. The examination system put a premium on scholasticism which, especially in later times, became almost a fetish with momentous results to art as well as to every aspect of life. The first great historiographers began their detailed records of the dynasties. Their successors continued them for two thousand years without break to give China the most completely documented history of any nation.

Granted that they sometimes require careful interpretation since they were written by the victors, no country has preserved comparable records of its past. In every field of government, trade, politics and art, a virile people made experiments which gave China a culture comparable to that emanating from Rome at the same period.

HAN DYNASTY – EAGLE – RUBBING –
CARVED STONE (H. 9 1/4″. W. 8 5/8″)

In the same measure that western civilisation springs from Greece and Rome, the civilisations of the Far East owe their inspiration in the first place to Han China.

Superstition and occult practices springing from Taoism went hand-in-hand with logical thought and the search for knowledge. The first hints of Buddhism, the Indian religion which was to change the whole pattern of Chinese life, reached China during the Han centuries. The Emperors were as eager to learn about this as they were to discover the Taoist elixir of immortality. Intellectual curiosity was one of the main features of Han culture.

For all its grandeur, little enough remains of Han art by which to judge its achievements. This is particularly true of painting. Wall-painting, one of the few forms in which Chinese painting approaches European, must have been widely practised. The few which have been preserved from old tombs give evidence of a developed style, a grasp of composition, a naturalistic skill in depicting individuals and a wide imagination. In breaking free from symbolism and conventionality, Chinese painting seems suddenly to burst into vivid life.

18

So few of these murals have survived that historians are forced to turn for evidence of painting styles to the more durable reliefs on stone or brick which decorate the mortuary shrines of the period. How far we are justified in drawing conclusions from them is open to argument ; they were probably taken from painted models and literary records suggest that actual paintings were very much more skilled. Although one accepts them *faute-de-mieux*, to our eyes they are remarkable artifacts in themselves.

They reflect a completely changed mental outlook. Whereas hitherto man had been the victim of unseen, mysterious forces, he now begins to domi-

HAN DYNASTY — LANDSCAPES WITH MEN HARVESTING AND SHOOTING WATER-FOWL — RUBBING OF A STAMPED TILE (H. 16 1/2″. W. 18 1/8″) — PRIVATE COLLECTION, CHÊNG-TU, SZECHWAN

nate the scene and to see the world about him with confident eyes. The everyday life and the rich legends of China are freely interpreted. Thus, the themes of art were greatly expanded.

The reliefs show him in battle or being entertained, engaged in industry or riding splendidly in swift, thin-wheeled chariots drawn by powerful horses. For the first time we have pictorial evidence concerning life in ancient China; the buildings, the divinities and spirits in which the Han Chinese believed and even their favourite animals. An eagle (pl. 18) is caught in a moment of hovering flight, wings outstretched in an arc, claws tucked up into its body, eye and beak ready to strike. The Chinese have always stressed the necessity for an artist to capture the "essence" of his subject. The powerful, alert glide of the king of birds is a typical example of this Chinese quality. The same spirit animated the Han artists as the bamboo and flower painters of the next two thousand years.

*The Horse* in pl. 23, probably a winged horse, is a strange mixture of myth and reality. He shows the same dignified qualities with which the Chinese endow their horses throughout centuries of painting. Its thick short mane and powerful body is the same as in the horse painted some seven hundred years later (pl. 42), in the T'ang dynasty.

A rubbing of a relief on brick found in Szechwan Province, West China, (pl. 19), shows a composite hunting and harvesting scene. It demonstrates how such mundane activities have become legitimate subjects for art and sweep away the old themes. Man is at one with nature. A powerful sense of movement infuses the work. Archers crouch with bows fully drawn ready to let fly at the birds which scatter in all directions in a most naturalistic flurry. Flat fish bask in the shallows beneath the large leaves of water plants. Below this, harvesters scythe the crops with an almost audible rhythm. A fellow worker brings food. How different is this from the hunting scenes on the earlier bronze in plate 15! It is as if the Chinese really begin to see for the first time. A sense of innovation, experiment and spontaneity common to all original artistic invention enlivens every line. All the limitations of the earlier bronze relief have been shed.

The spacing of the various elements is most carefully thought out to produce a definite sense of recession. It is frequently said that the Chinese do not concern themselves with perspective as we in the west understand it, but it would be wrong to say that they were not interested in the problems of representing space. Their concern is very evident here.

These artists were mainly interested in creating a clear-cut design which catches the spirit of men in action with a spontaneity and freedom of line to which we shall often refer. Even in these early reliefs a graceful sense of

20

movement unites and enlivens the scenes. No simpler or more satisfying design can be imagined than *The Rain* in pl. 22. A bare tree sways in the wind. Two women holding umbrellas repeat the bend of the tree while a few birds, caught in the storm, fly towards the centre. This is the art of silhouette at its most effective. It shows the combination of refinement and strength which are the main characteristics of Han art. The calligraphic line of the original paintings from which the reliefs were copied is very evident. They have a charm which is essentially "unstudied", but there is nothing in any way "primitive" about them.

The seeming effortlessness of the designs, which always surprises the westerner confronted with Chinese painting, is seen here in one of its earliest manifestations. It can perhaps be attributed to the deep effect of *Taoism* on their way of thought. For the Taoist "non-action" is the prime virtue. He

21

emphasizes the passiveness of the female which conquers the male, the softness of water which wears away the hardest stone, the use of "emptiness" as, for instance, when it is pointed out that the holes in a house (i.e. the doors and windows) are the really valuable parts. This idea of calm emptiness and humility influenced the Chinese approach to painting and especially to landscape. Above all, *Taoism* inculcated the ideal of the harmony which should exist between man and nature.

To reinforce the evidence provided by these many reliefs, a number of actual paintings on tomb walls have survived from the Han period. One of the most important is reproduced in plate 21. It was painted on sections of the pediment and lintel of a doorway to a tomb chamber and is now in the Museum of Fine Arts, Boston. The subject is an animal fight and a group of men shown as if in conversation. They are executed in ink and colour on a white background, the dark outlines being filled in with colour washes. Apart from the obvious skill of draughtsmanship and the lifelike spacing, the most outstanding quality is the striking characterisation of the individual figures. This is a remarkable

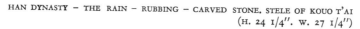

HAN DYNASTY — THE RAIN — RUBBING — CARVED STONE. STELE OF KOUO T'AI
(H. 24 1/4″. W. 27 1/4″)

22

HAN DYNASTY – HORSE – RUBBING (H. 19 3/4″. W.23 5/8″)
SZECHWAN PROVINCIAL MUSEUM, CHÊNG-TU.

feature in so far as portraiture is not the field of painting in which the Chinese rose to their greatest heights.

The Han dynasty was a period in which the force of individual personality counted for much. It was a valiant epoch of personal courage and opportunity. At the same time the state needed organisation and Confucianism with its emphasis on order and reverence for tradition was the most useful tool to forge it. But Confucianism as well as being rationalistic was also an intensely humanistic creed. These reliefs and wall paintings show how in Han times man and myth divide the stage equally.

The difference between classical Chinese art of the bronze age and that of the Han period is as great as between the arts of Egypt and Greece. The artistic discoveries of the Han period can be summed up in two words—freedom and harmony.

23

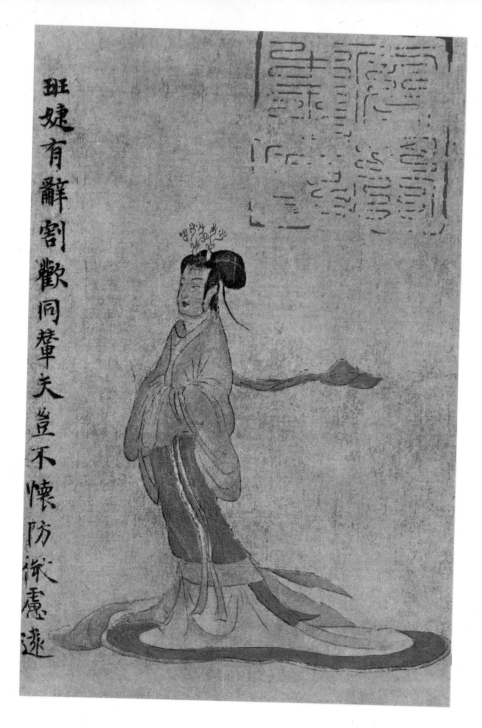

KU K'AI-CHIH (CIRCA 344-405) – ADMONITIONS OF THE INSTRUCTRESS TO THE PALACE LADIES –
DETAIL OF A LONG SCROLL (H. 9 7/8″) – INK AND COLOUR ON SILK – LONDON, BRITISH MUSEUM

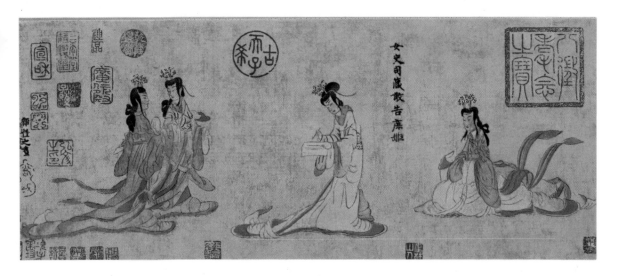

KU K'AI-CHIH (CIRCA 344-405) – ADMONITIONS OF THE INSTRUCTRESS TO THE PALACE LADIES – DETAIL OF A LONG SCROLL
(H. 9 7/8". W. 136 5/8") – INK AND COLOUR ON SILK – LONDON, BRITISH MUSEUM

# THE
# SIx DYNASTIES
## 265 - 581

A FTER the fall of the Han dynasty in 220 A.D. China split into a number of
independent states. The long so-called Six Dynasties period lasted from
265 until the reunification of the country under the Sui Dynasty in 581.
These three hundred years have been compared with the " Dark Ages of " European history. But most dark ages have their brighter spots and, in the North-
East, the Tartar tribes which had invaded China recognised the superiority of
Han culture and were comparatively rapidly transformed and absorbed by it ; in
the south, Han traditions were kept alive. During these years of anarchy,
few rulers of worth appeared, thrones were occupied by force and the dynasties
which opportunists created seldom outlasted their founders. The cultural
achievements of the Han were obscured in the turmoil but never completely
forgotten.

The period saw some important innovations. New blood from the North
reinvigorated the Chinese race. The Northern Wei dynasty, for instance, were
of Tungusic stock. The dynasty they founded in the border areas lasted from
386-557. A.D. They intermarried with the Chinese, adopted Chinese customs

25

and language and before long were priding themselves on being the preservers of Han culture. They adopted and encouraged the Buddhist faith; the vast cave temples which they hewed out of the cliffs and filled with myriads of religious carvings are among the artistic glories of mankind comparable to the Egyptian pyramids and the buildings of Ankor. The Liang dynasty in the South (A.D. 502-557), was likewise an oasis of Chinese culture and of the Buddhist faith. In order to understand later Chinese art, it is important to appreciate that during these centuries the south of China, which, although it produced poets like Ch'ü Yüan, had hitherto been considered almost barbaric, was now brought more fully into the orbit of Chinese culture. Some of our most valuable evidence of Han art has been discovered in places like Szechwan and in Korea far removed from the centre of Chinese culture. The troubled times fostered among intelligent men the Taoist ideal of retirement from the world, sometimes to a hermitage on the mountains, later under the influence of Buddhism, to a monastery. There they might escape the dangers and miseries surrounding them. This concept of escape remained an ideal of scholar and artist for the next thousand years. Sometimes it was a sincere belief, sometimes little more than an affectation.

The two main intellectual currents of the time were Taoism and Buddhism. Both made a greater appeal to the general population than the dry, exclusive ethics of Confucianism. Taoism developed from a profound philosophy into a popular religion, engrossed in the search for immortality and the philosopher's stone. Buddhism, one of the world's great religions, offered man immortality for his soul in return for leading a good life along the lines of simple faith, sacrifice and pacifistic ideals. It has been said of Buddhism that it is "the only foreign element in the Chinese culture which has penetrated every class of society, maintained its hold over long centuries and become accepted as an essential part of the national civilisation.[4]" Its metaphysical beliefs and its vast pantheon of gods and demi-gods inspired the artists of the following centuries to some of their finest works.

Alack, from these centuries also, little has remained to cast a clear light on the painting of the time. Paintings are as rare as from the Han dynasty. This is particularly unfortunate since the literary records abound with biographies of great painters and lists of their works. Why has so little survived? The two main centres of culture in the Northern Wei and the Liang both came to violent ends at the hands of less culturally minded men. The last emperor of the Liang, when his capital was threatened, consigned his whole collection of books, and possibly paintings, to the fire. The records of the number of books and paintings destroyed vary between 140,000 and 2,400,000, of which only 4,000 were saved. This serious blow to painting was only one of many such disasters.

Throughout the dynasties, Emperors have prided themselves on their collections, and have scoured the country (sometimes with truly regal unscrupulousness) to obtain precious works. Some have been themselves most competent painters, and many have, for better or worse, patronised the art. Again and again on the fall of their dynasty, their collections have perished with them.

The writings on art which have survived from this early period have had a great influence on subsequent Chinese painting—in particular those of a fifth century writer Hsieh Ho. In his *Ku hua-p'in-lu* Hsieh Ho laid down principles or essentials of painting to which artists of succeeding generations have constantly returned for guidance. He claims only to have recorded them and that they were enumerated by earlier writers. The *Six Essentials* are :

1. Reverberation of the life-breath ; that is the creation of movement.
2. Bone method ; that is the [proper] use of the brush.
3. Reflection of the objects ; that is the depiction of forms.
4. Deference to types ; that is the application of colours.
5. The layout of the design ; that is the arrangement of positions.
6. Transmission and perpetuation ; that is the copying of [old] models [5].

The last four of these essentials are comparatively easy to understand. The second emphasises the necessity for good brushwork. It is the interpretation of the first essential which has exercised eastern scholars for well over a thousand years and western scholars ever since they first became interested in Chinese painting. Painters and theoreticians alike have concluded that in its broadest interpretation it refers to some divine spark which must animate the artist. Whatever form his art may take, only the expression of this quality can bring it to life. Such a profound ideal, developed so early in their artistic history, has had the greatest influence on Chinese painters of all ages. It has urged them consciously to seek something more than superficial resemblance, to try to express the life-force behind every object. As a consequence, the artist approaches his subject with that same respect and humility which is demanded of life itself.

One of the few paintings which does throw some light on the work of these centuries is a famous scroll in the British Museum attributed to Ku K'ai-chih. Ku K'ai-chih lived approximately A.D. 344-405. He was eminent in his own day and the wealth of literary records make him one of the best-known figures in Chinese art history. He was an official and famous as "a wit, as a painter and as a buffoon". It is interesting to note in passing how early in China the individual artist emerged as a personality from the ranks of crafts-men. The fame and social standing which artists so quickly gained are important features in the history of Chinese painting ; it was not until the Renaissance in Europe that we saw a comparable development so momentous to western painting. Ku K'ai-chih is, in a sense, the Giotto of China.

The British Museum scroll is entitled *Admonitions of the Instructress to the Palace Ladies*. It is in the form of a series of didactic narrative scenes illus-trating various moral precepts intended to enlighten the ladies of the Imperial harem. They are full of great interest and variety. One shows a lady refusing to ride in the same litter as the Emperor for fear of causing scandal or distracting his thoughts. The lady actually accompanying him in the litter seems uncon-cerned with such high-minded considerations. In another scene a lady places herself between the Emperor and an attacking bear which had escaped during a hunt. The fourth scene shows the ladies at their toilet and illustrates the dictum "Men and women know how to adorn their faces, but none how to adorn their character. Yet if the character is not adorned, there is danger that the rules of propriety may be transgressed. Correct your character, embellish it. Strive to create holiness in your nature."

Few scholars are now prepared to admit that this famous early painting is an original by Ku K'ai-chih. The general opinion is that it is an early and faithful copy—at the earliest dating from the early T'ang dynasty and at latest from the Early Sung period—that is to say anything between the wide limits of 600 and 1100. Nevertheless they all agree that it faithfully reflects the work of the master and that it is of major importance. It certainly grows out of the same tradition which produced the Boston paintings, but the figures show a marked advance on those represented on brick and stone of the same period. The dramatic sense of the artist is highly developed. He has made a genuine effort to deal with the problems of perspective, sometimes quite effectively. He has produced a stage on which his figures appear convincing and real. The groupings of the figures are very free and experimental and the various scenes tell their stories most convincingly. Lawrence Binyon, over twenty years ago, said that the secret of this painting lies in its "very profound and subtle sense of life. The artist's finely organised nature... creates a sensitive human form in its natural dignity, the supple movements of hand and wrist, a discreet look in the eye, or the intimacy of glances exchanged.[6]" There is a calmness, an ordered quality in this scroll which we associate with Chinese painting. The compositions are all simply conceived but worked out with great thought to the inter-relationship of the figures. The emotions expressed are all re-strained but peculiarly effective—intense without being passionate, highly intel-lectualised, stylised but alive with human touches.

28

The last scene of this scroll (plate 25) shows the Instructress recording her advice, we presume for the benefit of the two young ladies gliding towards here. It is the most graceful of all the scenes. The willowy principal figure bends forward slightly with her brush and tablet in hand, the embodiment of dignity and ease. She is graceful and in command but she shows that slight deference which was to be expected of an imperial servant. One is tempted to see in the meaningful glance of the two young ladies not quite the attention which they should be paying to the tiresome lessons of their teacher. The text says "Thus has the instructress, charged with the duty of admonition, thought good to speak to the ladies of the harem."

Plate 24 is a single figure which comes just after the first section of the scroll as it now exists in which the Lady Fêng, a concubine of a Han Emperor, saved her master's life by placing herself between him and an attacking bear. She trails behind the lady who refuses to ride with the Emperor. Her slender figure is typical of the pre-T'ang ideal of feminine beauty and closely resembles the tomb figures of the period. Despite a certain vagueness and serenity, she is a woman of real flesh and blood. The face is drawn somewhat to formula but the drapery flows round a real body and she has all the qualities of dignity and desirability befitting an imperial concubine.

Is it possible to arrive any closer to an idea of the painting of this period over 1400 years ago? Again we must turn to stone reliefs. A number of decorated stone sarcophagi have been preserved of which the finest is in the William Rockhill Nelson Gallery of Art, Kansas City. It is dated *ca.* A.D. 525 and is a document of the utmost importance for a knowledge of pre-T'ang art. The two longest sides of the stone case contain engravings which illustrate the deeds by which various men became paragons of filial piety and as such enrolled in the Confucian Hall of Honour. The respect which children should show their parents is one of the oldest and most respected virtues in Chinese civilisation.

The groups of figures on this sarcophagus follow one another in what appears to be a continuous landscape. Powerful scenery is created by the interplay of jagged formalised rocks or cliffs and undulating vegetation. Animals and human beings are skilfully placed in the countryside. Two deer play on the low slopes in the foreground. The placing of the figures within the landscape shows considerable skill in the way it helps to create an impression of recession, although in fact there is no middle distance. The relationship between the figures in intimately suggested by a glance or a hand gesture. The workman who executed these scenes, whether or not he had a painted model to follow, was an artist of sensibility. Such a graceful sense of movement pervades the whole work that it almost gives the impression of being an underwater scene. Currents of movement are created, caught up and carried round in a circular movement. The flowing line of the whole composition makes one forget how stylised are the various elements which make up the work. Indeed if such works were possible in stone what masterpieces on silk and paper are now lost!

A number of tomb wall-paintings have survived from these centuries but they are not available for reproduction. The same is true of the more important wall paintings from Tun-huang. This famous site of cave temples lies in the Far West of China at the gateway to central Asia. It was the first town of importance in China that the Buddhist traveller or missionary would reach on his way from India. The city was established in the mid fourth century and was active until the first half of the eighth century. Unlike in Yün-kang and Lung-mên, the rock from which these chapels were carved was unsuitable for sculpture. However, the walls were covered with paintings which are of significance for the evidence they provide of painting in these centuries. It must be said that the painting is provincial and at first strongly influenced by central Asian styles. One can trace the gradual process by which the Chinese put their stamp on the work. The earliest works belonging to the end of the fifth and the beginning of the sixth centuries are available only in poor black-and-white photographs and in modern coloured copies which, according to the experts who have had an opportunity to compare them with the originals, have lost much of their character. At best they show how the Buddhist faith vastly enriched the imagination of the artists. The whole pantheon of gods and demi-gods, the myths and legends associated with the various lives of the Buddha are dramatically portrayed. It is not proposed to reproduce these early Tun-huang paintings. The Chinese are at present working very hard on them and it is to be hoped that at some future date they will produce a comprehensive study. Three of the T'ang period Tun-huang paintings will be reproduced later in dealing with that period.

# THE
# T'ANG DYNASTY
## 618 · 907

THE T'ang dynasty (618-907), the second Chinese empire, sponsored one of the greatest civilisations which the world has produced. It was established under the leadership of Li Shih-min, a man of remarkable energy and wisdom better known by his imperial name T'ai Tsung. Although only sixteen when the short-lived preceeding Sui dynasty collapsed in 617, he established his father on the throne and spent the next years in securing his position, in defeating his rivals, and in warding off foreign threats. He ascended the throne himself in 627 and ruled until 649. Coming from a respected family, his claim to the throne was less disputed than it might otherwise have been ; his scholarly turn of mind endeared him to the administrative classes ; as a patron of the arts he established the tenor of the whole three hundred year period.

The finest era of these three centuries of the T'ang was until the middle of the 8th century. The power of Chinese arms was felt further than in the Han. Chinese products reached the middle-east and western goods flowed into China. In A.D. 755 a rebellion by An Lu-shan administered a shock to the regime from which it never fully recovered. Although the revolt was finally defeated, the effective centralised control of the administration could never be fully restored and the provincial generals who had mainly been responsible for suppressing the revolt took an increasing part in the control of the state, thereby weakening it.

C. P. Fitzgerald says "In the T'ang period, an age at once more refined than the preceeding Han Empire and less sophisticated than the Sung Dynasty which followed, Chinese civilisation attained a harmonious balance between Confucian objectivity and Taoist introspection which was an ideal atmosphere for the cultivation of the arts.[7]" Economically the country had never been so prosperous or well organised. At its height of power, the taxpaying population alone numbered nearly fifty-three millions and Ch'ang-an the most brilliant capital of the contemporary world, housed about one million people. The religious and intellectual atmosphere of the country was extremely liberal. An open-minded and curious court welcomed foreigners; new religions such as Mohamadenism, Manicheism, Nestorian Christianity and, of course, Buddhism were free to practise and proselitize at least until the middle of the 8th century.

31

PAINTING FROM TUN-HUANG – TEJAPRAHBA BUDDHA AS SUBDUER OF THE FIVE PLANETS (DATED 897)
INK AND COLOUR ON SILK (H. 27″. W. 20 3/8″) – LONDON, BRITISH MUSEUM, STEIN COLLECTION

The period is best known perhaps for its poetry which flowed from the pens of such great writers as Li Po, Tu Fu, Mêng Hao-jan, Wang Wei and Po Chü-i. Even in translation it has captured a large western audience. Prose writers like Han Yü (768-824) established standards which have been admired and copied through the ages. Innovations were made in the drama, Buddhist theology, Confucian history writing and even in fiction which later generations were to build on. For a thousand years the Chinese looked back on the T'ang as their golden age.

Without doubt the most vital religious and intellectual force of the age was Buddhism. India, its birth place, had beckoned to pilgrims and seekers after knowledge. Intrepid travellers like the monk Hsüan-tsang (7th century) had spent many years there, touring the most famous holy places, collecting works of art and above all manuscripts concerning the faith. On their return they spent the rest of their lives in translating them and in imparting their knowledge to an eager public. The number of sects multiplied as contacts with India became more frequent and the distinctions worked out by the subtle Indian religious mind were transmitted to China. Each sect gained its followers. One stressed the importance of magic spells and rituals, another the more intellectual side of the faith, one emphasised the necessity of severe monastic rules, another the pantheistic nature of the religion. The sect which had a great influence on art was that of the followers of Amida. The believer in this sect was not required to practise the austerities laid down by Gautama, the historical Buddha. He need only call sincerely upon the name of Amida, a lotus-born Buddha whose sphere was the western region, to be assured of eternal life in his Western Paradise. By the end of the T'ang dynasty, Amidism was the most popular of the sects. However, those with higher aims could, instead of selfishly seeking only their own spiritual advancements, devote themselves to alleviating the sufferings of humanity, and hope to attain the status of Bodhisattva. As patron deity of this ideal rose the figure of Kuan-yin, the Deity of Compassion. However, it must not be thought that Buddhism was without its enemies and free to expand unchecked. The jealousy of the Taoists, playing on the vanities of emperors, resulted in a number of minor and a few serious major persecutions of the faith. Strict Confucians, like Han Yü, constantly complained that the country had gone mad. But generally speaking, it can be said that the T'ang was the great age of Buddhism.

However, it must be remembered that China was never prepared to be merely a meek and slavish imitator of a foreign religion and its art. She accepted foreign ideas but her cultural traditions were too strong to be entirely swamped. Buddhism filled an important gap in the spiritual development of the Chinese but Indian art was rapidly transformed and then passed on to

Japan, Korea, Tibet and Indo-China. It was Chinese interpretations of Indian Buddhist art which were of major significance for the history of the arts of the various far eastern peoples who accepted them. The religious ideas of Buddhism, especially in its pantheistic *mahayana* development, inspired a tremendous output of religious art both in sculpture and painting. Many of the sculptures from this period have survived and give a brilliant impression of the artistic heights attainable when technical perfection and unlimited financial resources are allied to deep religious conviction. Unfortunately, almost all the religious paintings which decorated the temples of the capital have perished together with the buildings which housed them. They exist only in literary records where the names of their painters and lists of their works are preserved.

Two exceptions to this almost total loss serve to fill the gap in our knowledge—the almost deserted site of Tun-huang and some Japanese work discussion of which belongs to another volume. As previously mentioned, the oasis of Tun-huang occupies a position along one of the main pilgrim routes to India on the N. W. frontier of China. In the hillsides there, devout believers carved devotional grottoes on a huge scale. These were plastered and covered with paintings. In 1907 Sir Aurel Stein, on a visit to the site, discovered the existence of a cache of documents and paintings in a walled-up storage cave where they had been kept intact for nearly a thousand years. He contrived to extract a large proportion of the most interesting which were divided between the British Museum and the Indian Government. Soon after him, Professor Pelliot visited the site and brought back more of these documents and paintings which are housed in the Musée Guimet. With the help of these precious documents of Buddhist art, it is possible to trace some of the outlines of the developments of Chinese religious painting over these three formative centuries. The present Chinese government has recently established a Tun-huang Institute which is doing valuable work in preserving and publishing the wall-paintings of the site.

Tun-huang, though important, was essentially a provincial site. Thus, for all their skill and interest, the paintings found there generally cannot have represented the work of the finest artists who were employed in the capital. Nevertheless, many of the paintings are very skilled products. Some, however, are the final results of constant repetitions of themes which had become so conventionalised over the centuries that they had lost much of their meaning. Taken as a whole, one can trace in them the Indian and Central Asian influences coming into China and the process by which the powerful Chinese artistic tradition imposed itself on them.

The most immediate difference which strikes the spectator is the increased competence of the painters in dealing with highly involved and complicated

34

PAINTING FROM TUN-HUANG (IXth CENTURY) – AVALOKITESVARA AS THE GUIDE OF SOULS
INK AND COLOUR ON SILK (H. 30″. W. 19 3/4″) – LONDON, BRITISH MUSEUM, STEIN COLLECTION

PAINTING FROM TUN-HUANG (IXth CENTURY) – FLYING SPIRIT – INK AND COLOUR ON SILK (H. 20 7/8″. W. 11 7/8″)
PARIS, MUSÉE GUIMET.

scenes.    The huge *mandala* or map-like forms with the inhabitants of the various heavens and hells carefully organised into their ordained positions, required draughtsmanship of the first order.    Secondly, the individual figures show in every respect—use of colour, perspective, line and characterisation a great advance on the earlier works as we know them.

Plate 32 shows the *Tejaprabha Buddha as Subduer of the Five Planets*. It is dated 897 but many writers have seen in it strong traces of an earlier style. The five figures surrounding the last human Buddha as he rides over the clouds seated on a heavy bullock-cart represent Saturn, Jupiter, Mercury, Venus and Mars.    Here the *Mahayana* Buddhist love of paradise scenes is united with a Chinese tradition for paintings of the planetary rulers which goes back to the first half of the 6th century.    The colour, composition and fine drawing produce a rich and powerful impression. The *mandalas* are generally static compositions with the deities grouped stiffly around a central Buddha. Here a sense of stately movement is produced by the swirling clouds and the circular motifs of wheel, halo and grouping of figures. All is calm and benign under the aegis of the Buddha—even Mars in the right hand corner is held in respectful awe. But perhaps more immediately appealing are the single figures, the appreciation of which demands less knowledge of an involved iconography.

The well-preserved painting in plate 35 depicts *Kuan-yin as the Guide of Souls*. Kuan-yin, in Sanscrit *Avalokitesvara*, is the deity of universal mercy, who quickly became the most popular object of worship in China and in Japan (there called *Kannon*). Like the Virgin Mary in western Catholicism, Kuan-yin's powers in the relief of suffering are limitless. To quote from a Buddhist scripture translated into Chinese as early as A.D. 400 by one of the great missionaries :

> *If you hear his name and see his body,*
> *And then diligently keep him in mind,*
> *It will extinguish all your suffering.*
>
> *If a living being suffers disasters,*
> *And unending pain torments his body,*
> *Kuan-yin's wonderful power of wisdom*
> *Can relieve him of the world's afflictions.*
>
> *He sees in truth, he in purity,*
> *He sees with enormous intelligence,*
> *He sees with mercy, he sees with kindness.*
> *Ever pray to him, ever adore him*[8].

Originally a masculine deity, Kuan-yin later became feminised in China and Japan. Here some male characteristics are still preserved, as for instance in the moustache and beard. In other respects the figure is very sinicised. The deity in long flowing robes stands on a purple cloud which has borne him down from paradise. Some of the heavenly buildings appear in the top left-hand corner. The robes of the body are richly but discreetly decorated. Flowers float through the air and the flames which envelop the halo repeat the gentle sway of the body. The pose is gentle, the whole atmosphere calm and restrained. A diminutive female figure stands demurely to one side—head reverently bowed and hands together hidden in the voluminous folds of her sleeves. Everything combines to create the same impression of dignity and grace which we noted in the Ku K'ai-chih scroll and to this is added a deep religious reverence.

Arthur Waley claims that the works is certainly a tenth century copy of a seventh century original. The composition itself is closer to Sung ideals in its free arrangement of figures and its lyrical feeling. But the type of female worshipper definitely belongs to the earlier period. Similar figures are seen in many tomb objects and in contemporary paintings preserved in Japan. According to tradition her plump style of beauty, unusual for China, was made fashionable by Yang Kuei-fei, the notorious concubine of Emperor Ming Huang.

An even more vivid single figure fills a fragment brought back by Paul Pelliot which is now in the Musée Guimet (Plate 36). Such flying figures are frequently found in Buddhist compositions both in sculpture and painting from the earliest times. They enliven scenes which tended to be static with the heavier figures of the Buddha and his attendants placed in the centre as if according to strict formulae. These central figures gave the workmen little opportunity to exercise their individual tastes, whereas in the subordinate figures the Chinese talent for flowing line and swirling movement is very evident. Many of the secondary figures and in particular these flying angels and spirits are painted or sculpted with great sympathy and originality.

We must now turn from religious to secular painting which is the true world of the Chinese painter. Literary records abound in the names of great painters of the T'ang dynasty. We even possess formidable lists of their works. A few more originals have survived from these centuries than from the pre-T'ang period but they are only the most minute remnants of what must have been a vast output. In discussing the achievements of an artist, copies though valuable are deceptive and the laudatory written word is interesting but of small practical value. Again, it is dangerous to judge the work of an artist from only one original. The few ancient paintings which have survived the thousand and more years since the T'ang serve chiefly to suggest to us the glories which are lost.

One such is by Yen Li-pên who lived during the stirring first years of this great era. The biographies say that he painted religious scenes and records of notable events which took place at the T'ang court. We know him as a portraitist, a reputation which is due to the survival of a painting of *Thirteen Emperors* in the Museum of Fine Arts, Boston. This long scroll, despite its somewhat poor condition, is one of our most important documents of early Chinese painting.

38

YEN LI-PÊN (DIED IN 673) – EMPEROR CHÊN WÊN-TI – DETAIL OF A LONG SCROLL (H. 17 1/2″) – BOSTON, MUSEUM OF FINE ARTS

Yen Li-pên was a Chinese official of a type frequently encounted in Chinese history whose abilities as a painter were more admired than his political skill. It is not said whether he was appointed to the court for his administrative talents or for his painting but before he died in 673 he had reached the position of joint prime minister. He appears to have been a model scholar-official.

The long Boston scroll is divided into thirteen groups, mostly with three figures in each group. The central figure of each group is a full length portrait of an emperor who ruled during the period from the second century B.C. to the end of the short Sui dynasty. The groups are isolated and all except two are standing as if in a grand procession. No backgrounds are provided and no attempt is made to link one group to the other. The section illustrated here (Plate 39) is one of the seated figures and depicts Emperor Wên-ti (560-566) of the Chên Dynasty. He is seated on a low couch with two female attendants standing behind him.  One looks backwards over her shoulder as if to the pre-ceeding group but such a break in the rigid frontal pattern is rare.  The per-spective of the couch and the disproportion between the emperor and his atten-dants are true to archaic patterns.  The artist without doubt was a great draughts-man absorbed in the representation of how he imagined his noble subjects looked in their day.  His figures have a calm and dignity in keeping with their imperial office.  Their expressions are subtly varied.  Their robes hang natu-rally about their full bodies and the use of heavy shading to emphasise the folds over the knees of the seated figure is particular interesting. This, of course, comes from central-Asian painting but is a rare feature in Chinese painting and it was never developed to such a degree as in the west.

It is often said that the Chinese did not rise to their greatest heights in portraiture.  With a few notable exceptions, what has survived would appear to support this observation but a considerable portrait art of high standard must have existed.  It may have been considered the realm of the craftsman rather than the artist and as such not worthy of collecting and preserving. When the Chinese applied themselves to portraiture they could achieve great heights and one would expect of an era like the T'ang that this form of art would flourish.

Yen Li-pên has here concerned himself mainly with the portrayal of the characters of the various emperors.  Emperor Wên-ti, for instance, was famous for his *Taoist* researches.  By comparison with some of the other Imperial personalities remembered for their more practical turn of mind, his face skil-fully reflects the more philosophical bent of just such a visionary.  Figures like these need little explanation.  They parade before us with all the heavy gran-deur, the pomp and circumstance of the highest of all possible ranks.  The static quality of the groups is endowed with a dynamic force by the majesty of the portraits.  This rare scroll illustrates Sickman's characterisation of T'ang painting, "Dragons, gnomes, witches, and the whole rich world of the supernatural faded gently out in the full sunlight of T'ang rationalism, forth-right worldliness, and assurance.  The ponderous majesty of an emperor, the frail emaciation of an ascetic, the poised and well-groomed refinement of a court beauty, no less than the spirit of a high-bred horse, were challenging subjects which the T'ang artist attacked with confidence.  Their art is lucid, balanced and at once elegant and solid. "

West and east share a common love of horses.  Their representation in our art is familiar enough.  Since mythical times when Emperor Mu is said to have covered the country on his legendary steeds, the Chinese have endowed them with divine qualities.  They have always been considered of greatest economic and military importance and they have inspired some of the greatest monuments of Chinese art. Already in Han times the horses on the bas-reliefs show a splendid heavy animation. The imperial stables of the T'ang Emperor Ming Huang are said to have housed no less than forty thousand fine animals brought from the breeding grounds of Ferghana and Khotan. The models of horses discovered in T'ang tombs include many masterpieces. The Chinese poets sing of them in all ages; they envy their dignity and intelligence, their proud freedom, their unwillingness to be held in human control, their bravery in battle, their sadness at being ill-treated or neglected. The companionship they give mankind is the theme of countless poems. The Chinese have a more intimate knowledge of horses and treat them more as humans than we do in the West.

Han Kan who lived *circa* 720-780 is perhaps the most famous of all Chinese painters of horses. His name is almost legendary and countless works both of horses and figures are attributed to him, unfortunately with little chance of their being genuine. One of the few which do approach his work is that of a *Horse Bound to a Stake* (Plate 42). This most appealing study of the Emperor's horse "Shining Light of the Night" is covered with the seals of many collectors and has suffered somewhat over the centuries. Nevertheless, enough remains of its bounding line and spirited movement to stamp it as the work of a great artist. In general form it immediately recalls the studies of Han and later horses with its rounded, heavy flanks, short legs, powerful neck and skull-like head. To quote Sirén "It has the quality of great sculptural art". But it is more lively than earlier works in its movement and more realistic in the manner in which it tosses its head in anger at being tied. This is an animal with a very distinct personality. The artist has used shading most effectively to give the impression of powerful, tense muscles on its chest and to darken the muzzle and eye sockets. Chinese historians recount how Han Kan strove to express the spirit of these proud animals by direct study from nature. When the Emperor asked him why his horses did not resemble those painted by another famed court painter he is said to have replied, "Your Majesty's servant has his own teachers: they are all the horses in Your Majesty's stables." This simple remark is more important than might at first appear, for it was often quoted by later painters as an indication of the need to study animal subjects direct from life, to share their emotions and not to allow empty formulae to guide their brushes.

Another famous painting attributed to Han Kan, *The Cowherd* (Plate 43), is in the collection of the Nationalist Government in Formosa. This shows a pair of superb horses, one black and one white. A powerful foreign-looking rider is seated on the white horse which is almost obscured by its darker com-

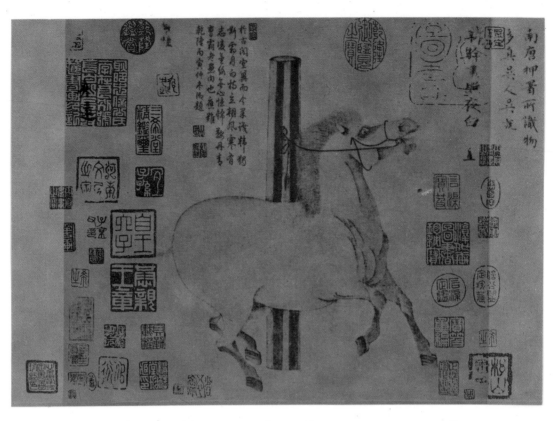

ATTRIBUTED TO HAN KAN (CIRCA 720-780) – THE EMPEROR'S HORSE " SHINING LIGHT OF THE NIGHT " BOUND TO A STAKE – INK ON PAPER (H. 11 3/4". W. 17 3/8") – LONDON, SIR PERCIVAL AND LADY DAVID COLLECTION

panion. A handsome decorated saddle is shown on the front horse. The colouring is soft and discreet but rich in effect. The tension in this painting is notably less than in the painting of "Shining Light of the Night" but this is perhaps due to the fact that the subject in itself is calmer and more restrained. The powerfully built horses here are made to share the interest with the ferocious looking rider who dominates them. The painter has conveyed an impression of restrained vitality. Although the horses have all the indications of high spirits—arched neck, stamping hooves and ears pricked up in the wind, they are not so dramatically conceived as in the previous work. Shading is used less noticeably but the outlines are firm and the drawing of the human figure is masterly. There is here all the dignity of noble steeds but any suggestion of their independence of spirit is absent.

These two paintings attributed to the same master are here reproduced to illustrate some of the fundamental difficulties facing the critic of early Chinese painting where examples by a certain master are so few that accurate comparison is impossible. Both paintings are well authenticated but they are obviously by different hands. Even allowing for the different media used this is evident. The *Horse Bound to a Stake* has been much restored but even so, its master was a less skilful draughtsman than that of *The Cowherd*. If the search for realism was the guiding force of T'ang art *The Cowherd* comes nearer to what we should expect of a painter who studied in the imperial stables. His horses are very close to the fine tomb figures of the T'ang; the master of *The Horse Bound to a Stake*, however, has taken his inspiration from pre-T'ang times. It is not the result of close observation but of inspired imagination. Conversely *The Horse Bound to a Stake* shows far more spirit. Although in places the drawing bears no relationship to the anatomy of a horse, the whole figure is inspired by a desire for vitality and freedom. The lines of *The Cowherd* are sometimes a little stiff and dry. It is not within the powers of the writer to say which, if either, of these two fine paintings is a genuine work by Han Kan but certainly they both reflect elements of his art.

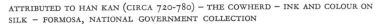

ATTRIBUTED TO HAN KAN (CIRCA 720-780) — THE COWHERD — INK AND COLOUR ON SILK — FORMOSA, NATIONAL GOVERNMENT COLLECTION

As we saw with these two paintings attributed to Han Kan, it is impossible now to assess with any degree of completeness or certainty the work of a T'ang Dynasty artist. Whereas the old histories and commentaries may contain an immense amount of information concerning him, perhaps only one painting of even possible authenticity has survived. Other paintings bearing the artist's signature may be good works of art but obviously not of the period, others are so palpably inferior work judged by any standards that they seldom serve to show anything more than the kind of subject he painted. It is thus possible often only to consider an isolated work and judge it in relation to its general background.

Chou Fang, for instance, who was active *ca.* 780-804 was one of the most famous painters of his day. He exerted a tremendous influence on his successors. He is said to have excelled in Buddhist painting and in portraiture and the critics praise his ability to depict the inner personalities of his subjetcs. He is most renowned for his paintings of noble ladies engaged in various activities such as making tea, walking, playing musical instruments and we are told, he even painted the famous concubine Yang Kuei-fei emerging from her bath, an intriguing subject which, alack, has not survived.

Such works are now little more than titles in lists. However, one painting by him in a western collection has some claim to authenticity. The Freer Gallery fragment of a scroll *Ladies Playing Sixes* (Plate 45) gives a clear idea of his refined taste and the elegant scenes he most liked to paint. On the right is a group of four obviously very relaxed ladies two of whom are playing a Chinese game which resembles chess. They are sharply characterised and absorbed in the game. Their gestures are typical and give the impression of a critical move about to be played. Behind the two seated figures are two spectators ; two serving maids bring in a huge jar from the left. The impression of effort in the latter is most subtly created by poise of body and arms. Here too there is no background. The figures are suspended in space and only their placing and overlappings create the effect of a solid scene. The drawing is delicate but assured. To judge from this, Chou Fang was very susceptible to visual experiences and, like many Chinese painters, a man of considerable sense of humour. He speaks to us in the same terms as many western portrait painters and he makes the same demand upon our own interpretative powers. The women who inhabit this picture are complete people and every aspect of their bodies contributes towards their complete characterisation.

Perhaps the greatest achievement of T'ang dynasty painting was in the development of a true art of pure landscape. Part of the credit for this must be given to the Li family who produced a number of outstanding professional

ATTRIBUTED TO CHOU FANG (ACTIVE CIRCA 780-804) – LADIES PLAYING DOUBLE SIXES – INK AND COLOUR ON SILK – DETAIL OF A SCROLL (H. 12 1/16″. W. 18 7/8″) – WASHINGTON, FREER GALLERY

painters. Li Ssu-hsün (615-716) and his son Li Chao-tao (died *ca.* 730) between them perfected a style of highly decorative imaginary landscapes in which the predominant characteristic is the use of brilliant colours—particularly green, blue and white and sometimes with the liberal addition of gold. These are the antithesis of the monochrome ink landscape style attributed to the other great name in early landscape painting Wang Wei (see later).

Plate 46 is typical of this style which Tung Ch'i- ch'ang at the beginning of the seventeenth century in his critique of Chinese painting called "the Northern Style." The painting has been attributed to Li Chao-tao but other critics, notably Sirén, believe that it is the work of a Sung artist faithfully following a T'ang original. In this dream-like landscape, a group of travellers, according to some *The Emperor Ming-huang on a Journey to Shu* wind their way through deep coulisses and mountains whose peaks soar into the heavens where clouds

cut and envelop them.    The emperor may be the mounted figure in red about
to cross the bridge in the bottom right-hand corner.    The painting is as highly
stylised as a Persian manuscript and a similar unreal atmosphere pervades the
scene.    Man is at one with a friendly nature whose giant features are arranged
as if they were the elements of a stage setting.    This is the kind of countryside
the poets could write about and reflects the pleasure and confidence with which
they made their excursions through a peaceful land.    The spectator is induced
to share the delights of a landscape which is painted in warm colours and bathed
in soft light.    The composition, though developed, still belongs to the same
fundamental approach as seen in the landscapes incised on pre-T'ang sarcophagi.
The style, a combination of imaginative interpretation and poetic statement,

SCHOOL OF LI SSU-HSÜN AND LI CHAO-TAO (7th OR 8th CENTURY) – THE EMPEROR MING-HUANG ON A JOURNEY TO SHU
COLOUR ON PAPER – FORMOSA, NATIONAL GOVERNMENT COLLECTION

46

is probably a union of this profane art and the scenes of paradise developed by the Buddhist painters. Thus the Li School were at once both traditionalists and innovators—the ideal of Chinese artists. The work greatly influenced many generations of Chinese and Japanese painters into the 19th century despite the calumnies heaped upon them by the amateur painters in monochrome.

Although the work of many of the most famous early artists has now disappeared, their traditions have been kept alive by countless later painters. The influence on later painting of Wu Tao-tzu, for instance, has been tremendous. It is doubtful if any artist from about the 15th century onwards ever saw a genuine work by this almost legendary painter but every one would know what his art stood for and when an artist painted in the style which he thought was that of the great Wu, he would quote from him or say that he was inspired by him. Western art shows no comparable feature.

Wu Tao-tzu is the only master who is said to have satisfied all of Hsieh Ho's Six Essentials. He was born about 680 and was one of the brightest stars at the brilliant court of Emperor Hsüan-tsang. Most of his work was in religious wall-paintings in the many temples of the capital. Many of these disappeared in the extensive persecution of Buddhism of 841-859 in which some 4,600 temples and 40,000 shrines were destroyed. His figure paintings were considered one of the greatest achievements of an altogether sparkling age. The praise which historians lavish on his discoveries and innovations in the art of depicting plastic form and movement remind one of the achievements claimed for Leonardo and Michelangelo. His compositions and the manner in which he placed his figures in space were, we are told, particular striking. The speed and strength of his brush are legendary ; he stands at the head of the long line of Chinese painters who based their technique on deep inward contemplation followed by rapid execution.

A few stone engravings after his work exist but to illustrate his achievements we reproduce part of a scroll now in the Osaka museum which is known as *Human Sinners Before the Judge of the Dead* (Pl. 48). Although it is generally admitted that this is a work of a much later century it preserves intact those qualities which are always associated with Wu's artistic gifts—vivid movement produced by free running brushwork and a striking arrangement of figures in space. As Taine said of Rubens, "he appreciated... the instantaneous movement which it is the aim of the plastic arts to seize on the wing." His personages are "suspended on the verge of action." In this impressive detail one sees clearly displayed the gifts for characterisation which are another aspect of Wu Tao-tzu's art. Each personage has his or her own strongly differentiated

AFTER WU TAO-TZU (BORN CIRCA 680) – HUMAN SINNERS BEFORE THE JUDGE OF THE DEAD – DETAIL OF A LONG SCROLL (H. 14″. W. 132 6/8″) – INK ON PAPER – OSAKA CITY MUSEUM, JAPAN, ABE COLLECTION

personality—fierce, dignified, compassionate, terrifying. And all are welded into a whole by the unifying power of his line and the harmony of composition. Above all the picture reflects the characteristic for which he was most famous and which has remained the aim of every painter—the expression through the brush of Hsieh Ho's first principle—*ch'i-yün*. Wu Tao-tzu was one of the most typical products of his time and people. In his art one side of the Chinese pictorial spirit culminated and was fixed.

Finally in this survey of T'ang painting we must consider the creation of the art of monochrome landscape. In its ultimate refinement a few centuries later, it is considered China's greatest contribution to the fine art of the world. The Chinese credit it to another of the now almost legendary T'ang masters. His name is echoed down the centuries but again his work cannot now be fully evaluated. Wang Wei (699-759) was the Chinese ideal of a completely cultured gentleman equally at home in many arts. He was a poet, musician, scholar, half official-half recluse and above all a great lover of the countryside. The style he is said to have originated differed radically from the paintings of the Li family and their followers (Plate 46) in which the shapes and colours of nature are so minutely described. He and his many thousands of followers of what later scholars called the Southern School used mainly ink in a free spontaneous manner. But landscape painting in this medium presented many problems, the solution of which gave Chinese landscape painting its distinctive character. It emphasized still more strongly the dominant virtues of outline and brushwork,

48

it led to a complete exploration of the possibilities with ink, it created an appreciation of the value in a painting of empty space and created a vocabulary of forms to which the Chinese have added steadily throughout the centuries. Wang Wei initiated a form of impressionism or essentialism which seem to us extremely modern. We are told that he used "splashed ink" which already is a very advanced form of ink painting. This technique makes a great demand on the imagination and sensibilities of the spectator if he wishes to appreciate the artist's very individual vision of landscape. He must associate himself closely with the artist's inspiration. Wang Wei in the 8th century synthesised the Chinese love of landscape. Into the study of the nature which surrounds them the Chinese have put all the care which the west have lavished on the study of the human figure.

Wang Wei is particularly well-known for the purity and classicism of his poetry which has survived better than his painting. From his time poetry exerted an increasing influence on landscape painting. A few lines from a Wang Wei prose poem translated by Arthur Waley give some idea of his sensibilities and of the observation he tried to express in painting.

> "*Going northwards, I crossed the Yüan-pa, over whose waters the unclouded moon shone with dazzling light. When night was far advanced, I mounted Hua-tzu's hill and saw the moonlight tossed up and thrown down by the jostling waves of the Wang River. On the wintry mountain distant lights twinkled and vanished... We must wait for spring to come : till the grasses sprout and the trees bloom. Then walking together in the spring hills we shall see the trout leap lightly from the stream, the white gulls stretch their wings, the dew fall on the green moss...*"

A further hint of Wang Wei's reputation may be judged from a poem Su Tung-p'o wrote centuries later about a painting by Wang Wei which he saw :

> *About the temple gate are clumps of bamboos ;*
> *Snow clings to the joints, hoar-frost whitens the roots,*
> *The stalks cross in seeming confusion*
> *And countless leaves are swayed by icy winds.*
> *But each brush-stroke is clear and precise*
> *And has its perfect part in the great design...*[10].

Plate 50 is taken from an early version of a scroll by Wang Wei *Clearing After Snowfall on the Mountains Along the River.* Although at second hand, it illustrates the lucidity and ordered quality of Wang Wei's work which Su

Tung-p'o praises. All the elements of monochrome landscape painting are here seen in their undistorted form; clear silhouette, strong brushwork, the effective use of empty space. We see the beginnings of types for trees and crevices, rocks and mountains. Even at this early period every stroke is digested. Above all he transformed landscape from the matter-of-fact world or from the fairy-land of fantasy to a plane of the spirit. And this he achieved without any loss of its reality. As one would gather from poems and biographies, snowscapes were a popular subject for Wang Wei and admirably suited to monochrome methods. Wang Wei, it can be seen even from this copy, has captured the atmosphere of silence and stillness over the country after a fall of snow. He is in complete harmony with the nature he loved. The whole picture is atmospheric without being passionate, poetic without being sentimental, dispassionate without being disinterested; it shows all the qualities which set the mood for the future of Chinese landscape and set it on the path of purity and intensity.

AFTER WANG WEI (699-759) — CLEARING AFTER SNOWFALL ON THE MOUNTAINS ALONG THE RIVER — DETAIL OF A LONG SCROLL — INK ON SILK — OGAWA COLLECTION, KYOTO, JAPAN

# THE
# FIVE DYNASTIES
## 907 · 960

For just over fifty years following the fall of the T'ang dynasty, China was divided and in turmoil. Five short lived "dynasties"—little more in fact than military dictatorships—controlled various parts of the country. Here and there, in some of the provinces of the far west and south, centres of culture held out under the inspiration of fugitives from the former capital now in ruins. It is interesting to see how short was this period of disunity in comparison with the nearly four centuries it took the Chinese to regain their unity during the Six Dynasties period. Despite the political chaos, these troubled years were very active in the arts. In particular they saw the full flowering of Chinese landscape painting. As far as we can now judge it was a completely new form of the art that a number of brilliant artists perfected. Art in general became once more thoroughly Chinese. The exotic elements so noticeable in the T'ang centuries were by now completely assimilated and the Chinese returned to reap the rich harvest of their own artistic traditions. It was a period of complete balance between the vitality of T'ang and the quietism of Sung which was to follow. Whereas the T'ang had "a lively pleasure in and a keen enjoyment of the colourfulness of this world... a relish for the good things of life", in the Sung "spiritual self-discipline is the keynote, a striving to grasp the innermost content of all being, together with a deep reverence for antiquity... a flight into the silences of nature[11]". The half century between these two distinct ways of thought was an interregnum in which the arts developed along very individual and personal lines. The outstanding characteristics of its artists was rationality and self-discipline.

It is difficult to determine why, in these troubled years leading to the foundation of the Sung dynasty in 960, there was such a burst of creative energy. Perhaps the final collapse of the vaunted but decayed T'ang dynasty administered a shock to the Chinese spirit which was salutary. Perhaps the splitting of the country emphasised the importance of the individual. To put it more generally, China was perhaps overdue for one of the periodical renewals of spiritual energy which mark its long history. The division of the country prevented the expression of this energy through normal political channels. Sensitive men, who would normally have devoted themselves to the service of their country,

51

found themselves unemployed and turned to the arts. They sought safety and peace in the search for more lasting values as seen particularly in the beauties of nature.

However, these men were nurtured in the afterglow of the achievements of the T'ang dynasty. Its literature continued to inspire them. The lines of the great T'ang poets, for instance, were common currency among men with any pretence to culture. The great early Sung painter Kuo Hsi (born 1020) in an essay on the Meaning of Painting says "It has been said by the ancients that poetry is a picture without form, and painting is a poem with form. Philosophers often discoursed on this topic and it has been my guiding principle. In my leisure hours, therefore, I often perused the poetry of the Tsin and T'ang dynasties as well as the modern, and found that some of the beautiful lines give full expression to the inmost thoughts of men's souls and describe vividly the scenery before men's eyes[12]". The keen observation and sensibility which the poets showed in the appreciation of nature must have acted as a constant inspiration to artists.

A few quotations, almost at random, from a few T'ang poets will illustrate their sensitive reaction to landscape. Li Po (A.D. 701-761) in a mood of awe writes :

52

*Above is the dark obscurity of heaven unfathomable,*
*Below the waves of the green water dash and tumble.*
*Heaven is high and the earth wide.*

Some lines from a poem by Ts'ui Tu express a nostalgia which must have been felt by many educated men in these years of division,

> *Tethered to a body and exiled in a dangerous country a thousand leagues*
> *[away,*
> *This evening I am surrounded by wild mountain ranges covered with*
> *[lingering snows...*

Mêng Hao-jan (A.D. 689-740) writes of early autumn.

> *The trees are bare, the wild geese have flown to the south,*
> *The north wind is cold upon the river,*
>
> . . . . . . . . . . . . . . . . . . . . . . . . . . . . . . .
>
> *I see a lonely sail upon the horizon and would like to follow it,*
> *Lost at the ford, I wish to ask the way.*
> *But there is only the vast expanse of water and the night coming down.*

TUNG YÜAN (ACTIVE CIRCA 1000)
LANDSCAPE – INK ON PAPER (H. 57″. W. 64″) – FORMOSA, NATIONAL GOVERNMENT COLLECTION

Farewells to friends inspired many poems. Wang Ch'ang-ling, in a poem devoted to this theme, says,

> *"With to-day's dawn I bid farewell to my friends, for I go*
> *to where the mountains of Ch'u stand isolated against the sky..."*

We see such subjects repeated in paintings throughout all subsequent centuries. In a poem entitled *The Hut by the Mountain Stream*, Liu Tsung-yüan

(A.D. 773-819) consoles himself on exile with the words : "*By chance I became a guest of the hills and forests*".

The T'ang poets are full of the most evocative lines which must have influenced the landscape painters deeply [13].

> *Scattered clouds pass over the the T'ai Mountain,*
> *Rain falls at intervals on the Chung-t'iao ranges,*
> *The colour of the trees follows the pass into the distance.* (Hsü Hun.)

> *The evening sun crosses the western passes,*
> *And all the ravines are suddenly dipped in darkness.* (Mêng Hao-jan.)

The expression of such sentiments in painting was taken up by a number of men of genius. Suddenly a whole generation became conscious of the full technical possibilities of brush and ink. Ching Hao (active 900-960), Kuan T'ung, Li Ch'êng (active *ca.* 940-967?), Kuo Chung-shu (*ca.* 920-977) are some of the outstanding names. Whether they used the more familiar outlines seen in T'ang dynasty painting or the more impressionistic means of dots and splashes, they all tried to capture atmosphere and spirit in their landscapes.

We illustrate this group of painters with works attributed to two of the most famous, Tung Yüan and Chü-jan. Tung Yüan's main activity fell into the second half of the 10th century but he reflects the feelings of the whole century. He came from the southern, richer, more atmospheric part of China and the ancient records say that "he was skilled in the mists of autumn and far open views." He worked in both monochrome and in the coloured landscape style of the T'ang. At this time, however, there seems to have been no strict division between monochrome and colour and his landscape in plate 54 combines the two though with an emphasis on ink. It is said to represent villagers taking part in a festival for evocating rain. The large composition is well-balanced and unites the impressionism possible with ink and meticulous detail such as the tiny figures taking part in the festival. Man, it can be seen, is of very little significance. He has his true stature and hardly intrudes in the picture. The great humped hills roll down to the waterside, a few huts nestle on a promontory, high in the background two boats are as if becalmed upon the lake. The colouring in this portrayal of the majestic powers of nature creates a rich but sombre effect. The warmth of this landscape is typical of the way the masters of the 10th century approached their work with a mixture of love and awe. These noble works are the outcome of quietism, the longing for peace and escape which, in a troubled age, were the dominant sentiments. Such landscapes are grand but not terrifying. The spectator can associate himself with the scene and enjoy

CHÜ-JAN (ACTIVE MIDDLE
OF Xth CENTURY) – SEEKING
THE TAO (THE " WAY ") IN
THE AUTUMN MOUNTAINS –
INK ON PAPER – FORMOSA,
NATIONAL GOVERNMENT
COLLECTION

the peaceful experiences which moved the artists. Kuo Hsi who was born in 1020 formulated the attitude quite simply in his comments on landscape "Why does a virtuous man take delight in landscapes? It is for these reasons : that in a rustic retreat he may nourish his nature; that amid the carefree play of rocks and streams, he may take delight... haze, mist, and the haunting spirits of the mountains are what human nature seeks and yet can rarely find." (Trans. by S. Sakanishi.) Such paintings reflect that delight which the artists seem suddenly to have discovered.

The Museum of Fine Arts, Boston, possesses a magnificent scroll *Clear Weather in a Valley*, plate 52. This has long been attributed by early Chinese critics to Tung Yüan and accepted as such by western scholars, although recently other critics have considered that it belongs to the 12th century. Certainly it is one of the finest and most important early Chinese paintings in western collections and among the purest expressions of landscape in the history of art. But the composition is more poetic and the use of ink more sensitive and varied than one would expect of Tung Yüan's work if the former example is a reliable guide. Above all, the brushwork presupposes a more advanced degree of stylisation and whole work reveals a technical mastery, a more subtle landscape sense and a realisation of the possibilities of brush and ink greater than we saw in the previous work attributed to Tung Yüan. It is an altogether more subtle and more sophisticated painting in every respect. It seems only fair to confess, however, that our knowledge of the abilities of these early masters is too scant and the comparative material lacking for a judgement based on anything more than the vaguest terms. One is tempted, however, to agree with Sirén in attributing this fine scroll to a period slightly later than the 10th century.

With the name of Tung Yüan, the Chinese generally associate Chü-jan, a Buddhist priest active in the mid 10th century and whose work spans the late Five Dynasties and early Sung Periods. A number of paintings are attributed to this great master but historians agree on only one of them as being likely to be from his hand. It is a large hanging scroll (Plate 56) in the National Government collection, Formosa and entitled *Seeking the Tao (the 'Way') in the Autumn Mountains*. This grandiose composition is filled with detail executed in strong brushwork and rich ink. It gives the impression of having been painted from top to bottom with hills and crevices hanging down to a stream at the bottom in which are placed a few hidden huts. The approach is very naturalistic and atmospheric. An austere spirit pervades the whole work. Kuo Hsi writing in the next century said, "Discipline should give a picture dignity. Without dignity depth is impossible." Chü-jan, one feels is here painting from the depth of his experiences, making landscape a true mirror of his soul, and reflecting through it the perennial desire of the Chinese spirit to escape from the cares of the mundane world to the large, peaceful, all-embracing world of nature. The scant evidence suggests that he is a stronger, less emotional character than Tung Yüan.

What are the qualities which distinguish the work of these 10th century masters? The broad landscapes suddenly show a command of composition and detail not found in previous work as far as we know it. They are a combination of patience and imagination and, unlike the T'ang landscapes which give the impression of being painted from nature, they are the products of brooding spirits working in the silence and isolation of their studios. The distant views of massive rock formations tower to the very tops of the picture planes. The vision is completely new ; one is not tempted to explore these landscapes ; there is no intention to make man feel at home in them, and, where occasionally man

UNKNOWN PAINTER (CIRCA 907-960) – HERD OF DEER – DETAIL OF PAINTING IN COLOUR ON SILK (ORIGINAL : H. 43″. W. 21 7/8″) – FORMOSA, NATIONAL GOVERNMENT COLLECTION

58

intrudes, he is overwhelmed and lost. They are brilliant syntheses; austere, often sombre and sometimes even forbidding. Their dignity conceals their synthetic quality. The technique in these carefully thought out compositions is painstaking. Light plays evenly and sparingly over the whole picture while only here and there it emphasises a particular feature. Everything is to scale but the artists seem more confident in dealing with near rather than with far perspective. This gives the huge mountains in the distance the look of flat back-drops, and their facets of rock the impression of random architectural features. Yet there is a calm logic about these pictures which contributes to their grandeur.

Both Tung Yüan and Chü-jan are important figures in the history of Chinese painting for the great masters of the Yüan period constantly returned to their work for inspiration and Tung Ch'i-ch'ang centuries later in his history of Chinese painting took them as the founders of the Southern School, the great line of painting which embraced all the amateur painters in ink. All subsequent scholar artists or gentlemen painters paid lip service to the achievements of Tung Yüan and Chü-jan. The lasting achievement of the 10th century landscape painters was their sincere effort to find and express the inner reality which lay behind the formal appearance of beauty and their full appreciation of the powers of brush and ink.

The sudden surge in creative painting evidenced by landscape was shared by the paintings of birds, flowers and animals. Plate 58 is the finest example of Five Dynasties animal painting. It is one of a pair that possibly formed part of a larger decorative painting. Its companion piece was shown in the great exhibition of Chinese Art in London, 1935-1936, and was one of the most widely admired exhibits. This painting is in better state of preservation and reveals a command of technique which is most unexpected for the period. A herd of deer are seen in a deep, luxuriant forest. The proud stag has sensed an intruder and lifts his head. Some of the does have also heard the noise while others continue to frolic through the woods. The freedom of the deer in their rustic life has always appealed to the far eastern mind. The scholar, borne down by the cares of the world, both appreciates their liberty and sympathises with their sense of persecution by the hunter. The picture poses many problems for we know of none other like it. It bears some relationship to T'ang dynasty work as seen in a few screens preserved in the Japanese Shōsō-in from that date. The only other comparable work would be the tomb paintings from Ch'ing-ling which, though painted in the Sung period, preserve elements of an earlier style. The atmosphere is extremely naturalistic, the trees with their soft, muted colours and delicate tracery blend with the soft tones of the deer. The sense of hushed woodland stillness is conveyed in every line and colour.

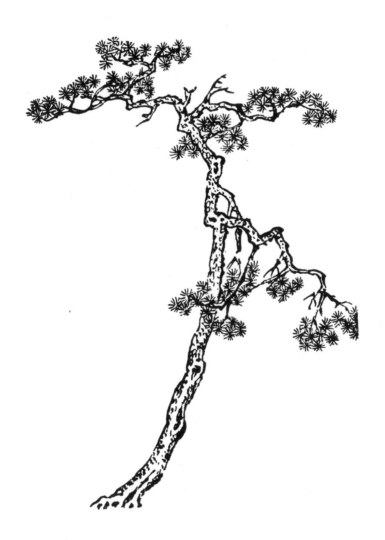

# THE
# SUNG DYNASTY
## 960 - 1279

WITH the decline and fall of the T'ang dynasty, China's greatest period of political creativity ended. It has been argued, with some justification, that the following thousand years can be thought of as simply the perpetuation of the great T'ang tradition. The boundaries of the country were formed; the colonisation of the tribes on the periphery of Chinese culture was well advanced. The framework of Chinese culture had been firmly laid down. The Five Dynasties, important though they were artistically, politically were only an interregnum; for the tradition of a China unified under a respected line had been so firmly established by Li Shih-min of the T'ang that no alternative was possible.

At first the prospects of the Sung Dynasty seemed no more hopeful than those of the previous five short-lived regimes. However, the first Sung emperor proved himself to be a firm man determined to restore peace. He broke the power of most of the provincial generals and re-established the centralised civil administration. But, even so, parts of the north and north-west remained independent. The people of south-east Mongolia were to prove a permanent threat, at first the Khitans of the Liao dynasty (907-1124) and then the Nürchen tribes who pressed down on them from the north, and under their own Chin Dynasty (1115-1234) crushed the Liao in 1124. In a series of wars with their more civilised neighbours, the Chins succeeded in driving the Sung Emperors to the south and split China in two. The period prior to this when the Sung Emperors ruled over both north and south China is known as the Northern Sung and the empire they set up after their defeat by the Chin is known as the Southern Sung (1127-1279). During this unhappy period the Sung tried to control the Chin either by ineffective wars or by bribery. We shall follow the usual custom of considering the painting of the Northern and of the Southern Sung separately.

The fundamental tenor of both periods was nevertheless pacific, introspective and intellectual, for the sensuality of the T'ang had disappeared in the troubles of the Five Dynasties period. It is significant that at this time Confucianism acquired a metaphysical background by incorporating ideas borrowed

HSÜ TAO-NING (XIth CENTURY) – FISHING IN A MOUNTAIN STREAM – DETAIL OF A SCROLL (H. 19″. W. 82″) – INK ON SILK

from Taoism and Buddhism. The system, prefected by the famous philosopher Chu Hsi (1130-1200), was based upon natural law, the "Supreme Ultimate" which was credited with the creation of the universe, through the interplay of positive and negative forces. The concept of this basic harmony of nature was one which Taoism had made familiar, and in Sung times it had the profoundest effect on the art of painting, especially landscape. "For the Chinese, the world of nature with its mountains, forests, storms and mists have been no mere picturesque backdrop against which human events are staged. The world of man and that of nature constitute one great indivisible unity. Man is not the supremely important creature he seems to westerners; he is but a vital part of the universe as a whole.⁴" As a force working upon artists, this new Confucian

62

attitude was reinforced by the outlook of *Ch'an* Buddhism to which we shall refer later.

In broad outline the painting of the early years of the Northern Sung period was a continuation of the styles developed in the Five Dynasties period. A number of great masters seem to have preserved and expanded their landscape traditions, though again direct evidence for the character of their work is meagre.

Our survey of the earlier periods of Chinese painting has shown how little remains of some of the greatest painters known to Chinese tradition. Occasionally, however, a masterpiece has survived from the hand of a painter about whom the records tell us little. A landscape scroll by a certain Hsü Tao-ning, for example, is one of the finest early paintings in any collection. We know hardly anything of its painter. He lived from the late 10th to the early 11th century and was possibly a chemist by profession. It can readily be seen that he modelled his style on that of the masters of the Five Dynasties. Kuo Jo-hsü, writing in the 11th century, says of him "Early in his career he set great store by a meticulous precision; but as an old man he cared only for simplicity and swiftness of drawing. With peaks that rose abruptly and sheer and forest trees that were strong and unyielding, he created a special school and form of his own." The landscape scroll in Kansas City, now only about half its original length, with its careful draughtsmanship seems to illustrate his earlier style. In an inspired flight of imagination, Hsü Tao-ning has created a strange mystical world which recalls the visions of some of our medieval western painters. With its rhythmical loops and sharp peaks seemingly eroded by countless ages, it gives the impression of a completely different world—a moonscape. The tiny figures in their fishing boat on the river seem desolate (Plates 62-63).

The strong rhythm which runs through the painting has led critics to compare it with a piece of music. It has the true genius of that unique Chinese invention—the landscape scroll, which adds the time element to painting. As the scroll is unrolled, section by section from right to left, the viewer is drawn into the world he beholds, and his participation in the artistic experience gains an added intimacy. As in music, themes are introduced and developed, abandoned and taken up again. A river disappears behind a cliff to reappear later in a different form, perhaps as a cascade, a path winds away behind a hill and we rejoin it in a changed scene—where we wander between jagged cliffs or where it leads us through a hamlet or beneath the eaves of a temple. Had the Chinese become interested in a fixed vanishing point or "scientific" perspective, such a progression would have been impossible. The variable perspective they employed enables the spectator to travel through the land with the artists, and without the western fixed view-point, the Chinese artist was able to achieve his effect of "far and near" by the use of mist and cloud effects, and by subtle variations in foreground and background whereby the eye is completely convinced.

An important name in the history of Chinese landscape painting is that of Li Ch'êng (active *ca.* 940-967). No originals by him have survived but he is famous for his gifts of depicting what the Chinese call "*p'ing-yüan*", "the level and distant".

Li Ch'êng's most eminent pupil was Kuo Hsi, an amateur painter-official who entered the Sung Academy towards the beginning of the 11th century. His *Clear Autumn Skies over Mountains and Valleys* (Plate 69) gives a clear impression of the ideal landscape painting of this time. From what he wrote

FAN K'UAN (ACTIVE 990-1030) – TRA-
VELLING AMONG MOUNTAINS AND
STREAMS – INK ON SILK (H. 77 1/4".
W. 38 3/8") – FORMOSA, NATIONAL
GOVERNMENT COLLECTION

he seems to have approached landscape in an essentially naturalistic manner but at the same time he emphasised the spirit which must inspire the painter's visions. To quote from his *Essay on Landscape Painting*, "How delightful then for a man to have a landscape painted by a skilled hand! Without leaving the room he finds himself among the streams and ravines; the cries of the birds and monkeys are faintly audible to his senses; light on the hills and reflection on the water, glittering, dazzle his eyes.[5]" A few powerfully-tensed trees take up the foreground along the near side of the river. The problem of the middle distance is conveniently solved by the blank expanse of water forming the river which leads the eye to the distant hills shrouded in mists. The cliffs, which to the western eye look so grotesque and exaggerated, are in fact a remarkably true impression of the peculiar land formations which the elements in certain parts of China carve from the loess hills. Kuo Hsi has here tried to go beyond the mere depiction of form and has attempted to capture the spirit of landscape. As a Chinese writer and painter of the early 10th century wrote, "Outward forms should never be taken for inner realities... He who tries to transmit the spirit by the means of formal aspect and ends by merely obtaining the outward appearance, will produce a dead thing.[6]"

In attempting to grasp the spirit behind the formal aspect of natural phenomena the Chinese artists evolved a system of types to which they added over the succeeding centuries and which in the end threatened to destroy the spontaneity of all Chinese painting.

We must now consider the other great Sung landscape painter whose name is coupled with that of Li Ch'êng, the master of "the level and distant". This is Fan K'uan (active *ca.* 990-1030) who is known as the master of "the high and distant". Like Li Ch'êng, he too was a northerner but, unlike him, he was of stern character and conservative taste. He drew the inspiration for his work from *taoism* and lived the life of a hermit amidst the mountains in order always to be in direct communion with nature. He never served the administration and remained a man of great independence of mind. The Chinese records speak endlessly of his great creative energy.

The finest of the few surviving works of this great name in Chinese landscape painting is an inspired landscape *Travelling among Mountains and Streams* (Plate 65) in the Imperial Collection housed in Formosa. The little party of travellers at the bottom winding their way amidst rocks and trees down to a stream are hardly noticeable before the huge rock face which towers above them. Here, too, man has his true stature before the grandeur of nature. The landscape is a true artistic interpretation of the scenery of the north of China and has nothing of the soft, atmospheric beauty of the south which was later to attract and absorb the landscapists. Apart from the overall grandeur of

66

concept and the dignity and bursting energy of the composition we see here two innovations which later landscape painters adopted and developed. He produces a new sense of form and solidity by the use of a particular type of dots and strokes *(ts'un)* which the Chinese compare to raindrops and he creates an impression of light playing over his large surfaces. Both seem spontaneous and natural; neither is overplayed. His reputation for portraying "the high and distant" requires no comment. The Chinese consider his work to be realistic but, compared with that of the T'ang Dynasty, we should be inclined to call it somewhat idealistic and emotional. It is something beyond realism and tries to reach into the spirit of nature and to portray its brooding personality. It is above all essentially Chinese; the epitome of the Sung vision of nature at one of its grandest moments.

It is interesting here to jump just over a century and see what happened to the innovations of Fan K'uan at the hands of an Academy master. The most famous landscape painter of the Academy at the end of the Northern Sung period was Li T'ang *(ca.* 1050-1130). He held high office in the Northern Sung Academy and most of his work was done while he was still at K'aifêng. He followed the defeated Sung Emperors to Hangchou and became the first Director of the later Academy but by this time he was an old man and few years of production remained to him. We are fortunate to be able to reproduce in colour his most famous landscape now in the Imperial Collection, Formosa (frontispiece). It is signed and dated 1124, just a year or so before the calamity which overtook the Northern Sung.

Li T'ang shows himself here to be in a direct line of descent from Fan K'uan but he was not exclusively devoted to landscape and he practised many different types of painting. His compositions range from large landscapes to figural scenes, genre subjects and even pictures of water buffalo. Taken together his work shows a wider approach and a less austere personality. This *Pine Trees in a Rocky Valley by a Turbulent Stream* is still in the grand Northern Sung manner and Sirén judges it to be typical of his middle period. Li T'ang has added to the heroic spiritual approach of such masters as Fan K'uan an increasing preoccupation with the techniques of brushwork. This interest almost dominates the picture. The stylised *ts'un* with which he denotes the stratified rocks are the direct antecedents of the powerful axe-like strokes which later distinguish the works of Ma Yüan and in particular of Hsia Kuei (see later). He was the most powerful influence on these later masters who shaped many centuries of Chinese landscape painting.

Li T'ang's view of landscape is closer and more intimate than that of Fan K'uan. As if to compensate for a resulting tameness he has tried to strengthen his vision by more powerful and consciously impressive brushwork. He is more completely master of perspective at all levels, in a sense he seems to try to combine "the level and distant" of Li Ch'êng with "the high and distant" of Fan K'uan.   In doing so he inevitably loses some of the qualities of both—the mystery of the former and the grandeur of the latter.   The realisation of this perhaps led him to introduce an element of fantasy which the earlier masters did not need.   In every way this landscape by Li T'ang marks a turning point— it is the final development of what Shimada calls "the effort to see landscape from within", the culmination of the study of the form and structure of rocks, the beginning of the lyricism of the later Sung and the preoccupation with brushstroke techniques.   If Fan K'uan can be called a realist, Li T'ang is here aiming at something more—a kind of supra-realism in which he tries to express the very inner structure of rocks, the geological bonds which hold them together. Li T'ang is the last great exponent of the grand manner and never again in Chinese painting is one to be so genuinely awed by the tremendous primitive power of natural phenomena.

The history of Chinese painting is studded with the names of outstanding artist who dominated their respective periods.   Though quite often genuine works by some of them have not survived, their innovations and styles

68

have become such a part of the rich living tradition that we can derive a very real impression of their genius. We shall refer to the practice of copying later in the text. One of the most illustrious figures in the whole history of Chinese painting is Mi Fei (1051-1107). Landscapes in his style by successive generations of painters would fill many volumes. His life has all the characteristics which would endear him to biographers and to the amateur painters who later triumphed over the professionals. He was an official whose dislike of chicanery and whose outspoken criticism caused his superiors to move him from one post to another. His judgement of painting was original, very independent and distinguished by a complete disregard for the unquestioned, oft-repeated praise which makes so much of ancient Chinese art criticism very dull. In fact he was eccentric in the extreme. He painted exclusively for his own pleasure, setting down his highly emotional reactions to landscape as the spirit moved him. He was thus considered the ideal *wên-jên* or gentleman painter—the gifted, intellectual amateur artist. It is understandable that such a man fell into disfavour with Emperor Hui-tsung. Mi Fei, however, had a posthumous revenge, for under a later Emperor, his style influenced the great academic landscapists of the Southern Sung academy.

69

Many works signed Mi Fei exist but modern art historians are unwilling to authenticate any of them. This is by no means intended to suggest that we have no idea of his highly personal view of landscape. Plate 71 *Spring Mountains and Pine Trees* in the collection of the National Government shows the classical Mi Fei formula. A few conical mountains in the background emerge from a very thick bank of white mist. The foreground is taken up by some pine trees in one corner whose lively jagged outlines offset the weather-worn mountain slopes. A hut emerges eerily from the mist. The simple composition is built up from a series of mounting cones. The effect is a view of nature in one of her many mysterious moods done in a way which, for lack of another term, we can only call impressionistic. This landscape is not so much intended to awe us as to linger in our senses. It is highly subjective, warm, human—the product of a poetic rather than a philosophical mind. It is the apogee of the concept of nature as friendly and harmonious.

The technique of ink dots and washes is no less distinctive. The drawing is reduced to a minimum and ink, often piled one layer upon another, is used in its most colouristic way. The records tell us how Mi Fei admired the culture of the T'ang dynasty—even to the extent of dressing in T'ang style. Little enough remains of T'ang landscape painting to show clearly whether he derived his style from it, but in some of the wall paintings in Tun-huang the conical mountains peering from the mist echo at a provincial site and in a cruder form a tradition which Mi Fei, through his appreciation of ink tones, may well have developed with great sensibility. Certainly his style is far removed from the crowded pictures of the 10th century masters with their wealth of meticulous detail and their emphasis on linear form. Landscape is here dissolved into a few basic elements expressed in a highly evocative manner.

If one can call the works of the earlier landscape masters heroic, those of Mi Fei are poetic. And since Mi Fei was an admirer of the achievements of the T'ang dynasty, this is not unexpected. Subjects from T'ang poetry still moved the painters—the impermanence of all things, the mystery of distant mountains, dreams by moonlight, a touching moment of farewell to a friend departing for some distant province, a profound appreciation of the changes of the seasons, impressions of the varied landscape of China as they made their travels, seeing here the sun setting behind the hills, there a ruined temple or palace, envying the peaceful life of a fisherman, being enchanted by a cluster of bamboos or a strange tree clinging tenaciously to the jagged rocks, encountering a monk or a woodcutter in the mountains. Above all we find reflected the poet's song of joy in retreating to the peace of the mountains where, in silent communion with the eternal, the cares of the world slip from his shoulders. All the emotions which the Sung painters tried to capture had been explored by the ancient poets and expressed in sensitive and highly evocative language. Mi Fei would have been familiar with such poems as that of Po Chü-i "Song of the Pines",

> *I like sitting alone when the moon is shining*
> *And there are two pines standing before the verandah.*
> *A breeze comes from the south-west,*
> *Creeping into the branches and leaves,*
> *Under the brilliant moon at midnight*
> *It whistles a cool distant music*
> *Like rustling rains in empty mountains*
> *And the serene harp-strings in the fall...*[17].

ATTRIBUTED TO MI FEI (1051-1107) – SPRING MOUNTAINS AND PINE TREES – INK AND COLOUR ON PAPER – FORMOSA, NATIONAL GOVERNMENT COLLECTION

The brevity and emotion of these paintings have led to his work being called "the most brilliant interpretations of the romantic ideals of the Southern School."

The figure painters of the Northern Sung period can hardly be compared either in originality or depth of inspiration with the great landscape masters like Hsü Tao-ning, Kuo Hsi and Mi Fei. The only permissible exception to this generalisation is Li Kung-lin (*ca.* 1040-1106) better known by the name Li Lung-mien. Like many a great painter before him, he was an official though he never achieved high office. The Chinese records praise him for his breadth of culture and his nobility of spirit. He was intimate with many of the great intellectual figures of his age such as Mi Fei and Su Tung-p'o. In all respects

EMPEROR HUI-TSUNG (REIGNED : 1101-1125) – FIVE COLOURED PARAKEET – PART OF A SCROLL – INK AND COLOUR ON SILK (H. 20 7/8″) – BOSTON, MUSEUM OF FINE ARTS

he was the ideal type of gentleman painter, the production of which has been one of the distinguishing features of Chinese civilisation.

As a painter he was a traditionalist. He had studied the great masters of the past, especially Ku K'ai-chih, Lu T'an-wei and Wu Tao-tzu. Han Kan was the inspiration for his famous paintings of horses and his landscapes owed much to the example of Wang Wei "Never for a day" it is said, "did he forget the mountains and forests". But it was his figure paintings which brought him fame and which influenced many generations of his followers. Although he came from an orthodox Confucian family, his paintings also included many

73

Buddhist subjects. It is here that we see the power of the tradition created by Wu Tao-tzu and, if one likes to go further back, that of Yen Li-pên.

We have seen that the traditional reputations of many early artists do them more credit than the works attributed to them which have survived. Despite his fame, the surviving paintings by Li Lung-mien, in the opinion of the present writer, seldom seem to justify his reputation. We see in them little of the spontaneity and individuality which we should expect of a master who said of himself "When I paint, I do it as the poet composes his poem; I chant my heart's desire and nothing more".

Only two paintings attributed to Li Lung-mien are masterpieces of the kind we should expect from such a vaunted talent. The first is the well-known series of horses in Japan. The second (Plate 72) is a portrait of *Vimalakirti*, the eminent disciple of the Buddha who visited him on his sick bed. The painting may, as many writers suggest, be of a slightly later date, but it has the qualities of a great artist. The noble figure in flowing robes is seated on a low couch gazing intently to his left. The piercing characterisation for which Li Lung-mien was famous, the flowing line inherited from Wu Tao-tzu, the clarity of spontaneous invention and above all the grace and control expected of a Northern Sung master are all present in this imposing composition. The bejewelled lady in the background emphasises the simplicity of the central figure. The carefully observed decoration of the couch acts as a frame to the bold sweeping robes of the sage and the swirling clouds in the background add an ethereal atmosphere to the whole scene. The bearded face stands out within its plain halo and even in such small details as the pair of shoes which cut the stiff line of the couch we see the work of a great draughtsman. The Buddhist spirit behind this painting is more relaxed without in any way detracting from its religious power. It is the essence of that love of line and movement even in repose for which Chinese painting is famous.

Another important type of subject in early Sung painting was in the field of flowers, birds and animals. I Yüan-chi, for instance, painted flowers and birds but is particularly well known for his paintings of monkeys and deer. He said that he took up these subjects because none of the ancient masters had attempted them and he hoped thereby to gain a reputation. *The Monkey* in plate 81 is typical of his work. A Monkey is cuddling a kitten while the mother-cat expresses her anxiety. The drawing is extremely fine, the colouring soft and the very human characterisation of the animals perfect. This, we are told, he acquired by long study of the animals in their native habitat. Such close identification of the artist with his subject is an important aspect of Chinese painting. Lin Yu-t'ang says of this "In order to paint a fish, the artist must understand the 'nature' of fish but in order to do so he must, through the

74

exercise of his intuitive imagination, mentally swim with it in the water and share its reactions to current and storms and light and food. Only an artist who understands the joys of the salmon in leaping the rapids and realizes how exciting it is to him should try to paint the salmon. Otherwise he should leave the salmon alone, for no matter how accurate the painting is of its scales and fins and eyelids, the painting will be dead.[18]"

I Yüan-chi was not a member of the Academy and court recognition came to him late in life when he was summoned to paint a screen for the Emperor (1064) and later in 1066 to paint a scroll with a hundred gibbons. He died just after he had started this great work. But the biographies of this artist are typically vague. They say he followed no particular master but appreciated the work of the ancients, that sometimes he painted very freely and sometimes in strict accord with the rules. Although Emperor Hui-tsung had some 245 paintings by him in the huge collection he built up few have survived and we know very little about him. Mi Fei, who was extremely difficult to please, praised him very highly and added that he aroused such jealousy among the court painters that they poisoned him!

Certainly, from his time the monkey became a most popular subject in the Chinese painter's repertoire. Mu Ch'i did a famous painting of a monkey now in the National Museum, Kyoto, Japan and such very attractive studies have been repeated down the centuries by Chinese and Japanese alike. The monkey holds a particular place in Chinese legend. In the 7th century Hsüan Tsang made his renowned pilgrimage to India in search of Buddhist knowledge. By the 10th century at least a whole series of fantastic legends grew up about this journey. The secondary character in this saga was the King of the Monkeys, a mischievous, lovable genius who is said to have accompanied him and to have helped him through his trials. Monkey became a favourite stage character and finally, from a mass of popular material, a book was compiled in the 16th century of their travels together[19]. Apart from this, monkeys are, like deer, always associated with the peace of the countryside. "The cry of monkeys" is a phrase which occurs in many poems to suggest the remoteness of a distant place.

Imperial patronage of painting in China has been a mixed blessing but it has certainly been a powerful force. It goes back to the T'ang dynasty. The first Imperial Academy of painting (Hua-yüan) was established in the first half of the 8th century by the Emperor Hsüan-tsang (713-756). This made official the practice begun even earlier of gathering outstanding artists from all over the country to serve the court. They were provided with the facilities to pursue their art, supported by good salaries and often heaped with honours. The Sung dynasty Academies followed the pattern of those of the T'ang but

75

the Sung emperors were themselves often painters of ability. The dangerous situation arose of emperors dictating not only the subjects but also the style which they expected of their academy painters. Emperor Hui-tsung (1101-1125), the last of the Northern Sung rulers, was a particularly determined controller of his academy. He provided the subjects for the entrance examination, demanded a rough draft of proposed works by academy members, supervised the work while it was in progress and passed the final product. The judgement of posterity has been hard an "official taste" but an academy of painting need not necessarily be a deadening institution. At times the Hua-yüan did, in fact, contain some of the most original Chinese painters like Ma Yüan and Hsia Kuei.

The style developed by the academy was in accordance with tastes of the wealthy to whom bird and flower paintings most appealed. These are generally small works in ink and colour. The general lines of this type of painting were laid down in the T'ang dynasty but during the Sung, after a short experiment in monochrome, the academy settled down to painting realistic works

76

DETAIL OF A LONG SCROLL (H. 13 3/8″. W. 183 1/8″) – INK ON PAPER – HONOLULU, ACADEMY OF ARTS

with delicate outlines, refined colouring and sensitive detail. The academy was always conservative in outlook, laying emphasis on the necessity to preserve line and brushwork. Such an atmosphere of conservation may have been influenced by the interest in archaeology at the time created by the discovery of ancient bronzes dating to the first millenium B.C. and Emperors of China anyway have always felt the necessity of preserving the past.

Hui-tsung was an artist of considerable merit judged by the standards of court taste. His *Five Coloured Parakeet* (Plate 73) is typical of Sung Academy workmanship but it is more than just the empty decoration into which many academy paintings deteriorated. The bird perched on its flowering branch stands out in crisp isolation. Space is used constructively—an approach absorbed from the great spiritual masters of this period. The weight and balance of the composition is most skilfully maintained and the whole picture breathes an air of natural harmony.

Why is it that Chinese paintings of flowers, birds and animals make such an immediate appeal to our senses? Fundamentally because, whatever tech-

77

nique they use, fine drawing or splashes of ink, the natural vision is always the basis of their art. Their creators have a deep love of all life and seem willing to abandon themselves to nature with complete humility. Chinese painting of these subjects is touched with a genuine wonder and they seldom intrude upon it for fear that man's clumsiness may break the spell.

ATTRIBUTED TO LI TI (CIRCA 1100-1197) – HERDSMEN RETURNING HOME IN A THUNDERSTORM – INK ON SILK – FORMOSA, NATIONAL GOVERNMENT COLLECTION

This reticence is seen in a work attributed to Ma Fên. We know very little about this painter who specialised in animals. He lived somewhat later than I Yüan-chi, serving in the Academy in the first quarter of the 12th century. We hear nothing of him after the flight of the northern Sung and he may well have been swept away in the disorders following the fall of K'ai-fêng. *The Hundred Geese* (Pl. 76-77) in the Honolulu Academy bears his name but critics do not agree that it is actually a work by Ma Fên. The signature seems to be a later addition. Some authorities place it in the late Sung, some in the Yüan and some even in the Ming period. The late Sung is most favoured. But lack of comparative material makes any definite decision impossible.

Each bird in this long scroll is an individual study in suspended movement, every gesture and pose is carefully built up to produce a variety which is never tedious. Starting from a group at rest, the geese enter the water, emerge from the mist in a long flight, check and settle down at the end of the scroll. The graceful arc of birds on the wing carries us with it in imagination.

Many painters attempted scrolls made up of a hundred animals. They are the greatest test of an artist's observation, ingenuity and draughtsmanship. But these powers alone are not enough. The Chinese painter must then weld these individual studies into a convincing unity and a dynamic whole. Few have succeeded as well as the artist of *The Hundred Geese*. The soft colours and the mist reproduce the cool, still atmosphere of early morning, the graceful birds contrast effectively with the angular bamboos emerging mysteriously from the water. Only a Chinese master could combine so effectively the naturalism of the birds with the impressionism of the bamboos. The tones are everywhere perfect. It is impossible to think of this expression of rapture in the powers of creation as a dry copy.

While the Sung court spent its energies in the intellectual and artistic pursuits which are its monuments, significant changes were taking place among the barbarian tribes in the north. The Liao Kitans, hitherto held at bay only by bribery, were replaced in 1124 by one of their more vigorous vassals the Nürchen or, to give them their Chinese name, the Chin. The Sung Emperor was understandably relieved at the defeat of the Liao, but rashly saw in this an opportunity to stop paying the heavy subsidy to his warlike neighbours and also to regain the territory lost to them. Unfortunately, he had not the means available to take advantage of the temporary division and he failed to appreciate that the Chin were still more dangerous than the Liao. The Chin turned upon the poorly-trained Sung troops, swept down into north China and routed the Chinese. The Chinese, who did not learn from this defeat, tried treachery. The Chin returned to the attack, destroyed the old capital of K'ai-fêng, and crossed the river to sack other southern cities including Hang-

SU HAN-CH'EN (ACTIVE ABOUT
1160) – CHILDREN PLAYING
WITH CRICKETS – INK AND
COLOUR ON SILK (H. 77".
W. 43") – FORMOSA, NATIONAL
GOVERNMENT COLLECTION

chou. Emperor Hui-tsung and some three thousand members of the court were carried off into captivity. Those who escaped scattered to the hills to await better times. It was not until 1131 that the remainder of the Sung troops could regroup under a capable leader and re-establish themselves in Hangchou. For another century or so, in the beguiling atmosphere of this beautiful lake-side city (praised slightly later by the Venetian Marco Polo as the finest city in the world), they had respite to pick up the threads of their old, refined life. Then the Chin and Sung together were swept away by the most devasting of all the northern raiders—the Mongols.

When Kao-tsung, the son of the captured Hui-tsung re-established the Academy in Hangchou he could call on a number of members of his father's Academy to form a nucleus which would continue its traditions. Life went on much as before, perhaps even more gaily and indolently than in K'ai-fêng for the lake-side city of Hangchou seemed designed for pleasure. The ravages of the Chin seemed to the confident Chinese as only an aggravated form of the trials suffered under the Liao. Yet it is tempting to see in some of the Academy painting of this time an escapism and a melancholy atmosphere which is the

1 YÜAN-CHI (ACTIVE ABOUT 1064-67)
MONKEY – DETAIL OF A PAINTING IN INK
AND SLIGHT COLOUR ON SILK – FORMOSA,
NATIONAL GOVERNMENT COLLECTION

reflection of the hard times and a presage of disaster. In the hands of sensitive painters these qualities created a peculiar wistfulness.

Li Ti (*ca.* 1100-1197) was one of the northern Sung masters who picked up the threads of court painting in Hangchou. He rose to become Vice-Chancellor of the new Academy. Little is known about him. He is said to have painted many subjects but he is best known for his rustic paintings with water-buffalo. Plate 78 *Herdsmen Returning Home in a Thunderstorm,* which is attributed to him, shows the technical skill, the charm and the artificiality of Academic art at their most attractive. Though we do not know when it was painted, the scene could well be set along the misty shore of the Western Lake in Hangchou. It is from the hand of a gentle and humorous man. Willows and bamboo thickets bend over in the wind. Two diminutive figures on heavy water-buffalo press their slow beasts to return before the storm engulfs them. The contrast between the agitated figures and the unconcerned, lethargic beasts is most effective. One has lost his hat and balances the wrong way round on his mount like a circus clown caught unawares on a ring horse. The segment of nature is small; nothing could be farther from the towering landscapes of the Five Dynasties. By comparison this painting seems an exercise in conscious rusticity, a set piece within a carefully laid-out park where the rustics play their simple roles for the pleasure of the nobility—a Chinese Arcady. It would be rash to read into these fleeing figures any deeper significance. But most court art, in one form or another, is by nature frankly escapist and by any standards this painting is an attractive and able work. The figures are real and the composition convincing. The soft atmosphere is strengthened by decisive brushwork. The appeal is that of the shepherd in western painting—the nostalgia for the simple life which has tormented sensitive men in all highly organised societies. The Chinese court painter is often saved from the sentimentality which this can create by a genuine humility in his dealings with nature and by an ability to associate himself very closely with his subjects.

This sympathy is seen in the work of another member of the old Academy who lived to work in Hangchou. Su Han-ch'en was still working in the 1160's and was particularly famous for his paintings of children. His charming subjects, like those of Velasquez, look more like miniature adults than children. His compositions have been frequently copied. Sickman said of the painting in Plate 80 *Children at Play,* " His children are all princelings who play in a wonderful world of palace gardens or whose every wish is gratified by the toy-seller, his cart laden with the marvels that fill the dreams of small boys... the picture is an intimate glimpse of the protected idyllic life fostered at an imperial court." In the painting two small children bend over a lacquered and inlaid table with the intensity typical of small children. They are playing with a cricket.  Another similar table holds the clutter of their abandoned toys.  The willingness of children to discard artificial toys for the pleasures of watching an insect is universal.  Behind them rears a strange-shaped rock with flowers growing round it.  The obvious contrast in form, size, colour, age and texture between the children and the rock is very effective.  The Chinese have always been fascinated by striking old rocks.  They would buy them, often at fantastically high prices, and sometimes carry them hundreds of miles to decorate the gardens of Hangchou.  Their love of childred is traditional.  The painter has combined youth and age into a nostalgic world of fantasy, and as this is an Academy painting, one senses that nostalgia and fantasy were indeed the dominant qualities of this twilight of Sung culture.

One of the most far-reaching spitirual forces in the long history of China is that of the *Ch'an* or "Contemplation" sect of Buddhism (perhaps better known in the Japanese transliteration *Zen*).  An Indian preist Bodhidharma is said to have brought the sect to China as early as A.D. 520.  It had a faithful following over the centuries but it was not until the twelfth and thirteenth centuries that the *Ch'an* interpretation deeply influenced the arts in a particularly direct manner.

The tenets of the sect are not easy to express in words—partly because the great *Ch'an* teachers eschewed all holy writings and emphasised that the way to Buddhahood could not be expressed in words.  Bodhidharma had laid down the basis of the teaching when he stressed the vital part played by intuition in the achievement of truth.  To this fundamental belief several other concepts were added, some either derived from or in harmony with the ancient Chinese stream of Taoist thought.  Its sources are thus partly Indian but the outcome was essentially Chinese.  Intense and often prolonged meditation was the means by which the mind could be cleared and prepared for the sudden flash of intuition in which man was to find the Buddhahood within himself.  Through meditation he could reach *sūnyatā*, the "great emptiness," the preparatory state for the achievement of union with the highest truth or "First Principle."

Significantly for the art of painting, *Ch'an* taught that the Buddha nature inhabited every aspect of nature, the smallest twig of the most insignificant tree as well as the most grandiose mountain, the tiniest of insects as well as the most devout priest.  This interpretation of the faith encouraged man to seek and experience unity with nature in its every aspect.  Thus the range of painting was immeasurably enriched.  *Ch'an* painting, in its deep interest in all created things, produced some of the most evocative landscapes, striking portraits and profound still-lifes in the art of the east.  Perhaps its greatest achievement was its power to make us see the mystery in the most common-

MU CH'I (ACTIVE 1200-1250) – THE SIX PERSIMMONS – INK ON PAPER (H. 14 1/8″. W. 15″)
KYOTO, JAPAN, DAI-TOKUJI COLLECTION

place sights of nature. "Here there is no formal iconography, but an intuition that has to be expressed in an ink painting where no least stroke of the brush can be erased or modified; the work is as irrevocable as life itself. There is no art that comes nearer to 'grasping the joy as it flies'... no kind of art more studied in method, or less laboured in effect. Every work of *Ch'an-Zen* art is unique, and in proportion to its perfection inscrutable.[20]" This highly abbreviated, intuitive, introspective art aimed at recording a moment of visual truth with the same immediacy as accompanied spiritual enlightenment; it produced the most outstanding mystical art of China and Japan. Late Sung painting thus achieved a balance which reflects itself in the attempt to discover "the internal relationship that exists between nature and self." It harmonised the

LIANG K'AI (ACTIVE ABOUT 1200) – CH'AN PRIEST – INK ON PAPER – FORMOSA, NATIONAL GOVERNMENT COLLECTION

outlook engendered by Neo-Confucianism which taught that "Everything in nature, including the self, is the manifestation of the universe itself" and that of the Ch'an Buddhist "Since the human mind is provided with the essence of the universe, the mind is the very universe itself.[21]" The impulse for painting thus came from intellectual sources. It was the period, to quote Grousset, of the "intellectualisation of the Chinese aesthetic.[22]" The tendency had started in the T'ang and perhaps even earlier with the introduction of Buddhism. From the 10th to 13th centuries it was completed.

The outstanding example of a *Ch'an*-inspired still-life is the small painting of six *Persimmons* (Plate 84) by Mu Ch'i, a priest-painter active in the Hangchou area during the first half of the 13th century. Most of his work has been preserved in Japan where it has greatly influenced Japanese painters of later generations. Sickman says of this elusive work, "Few other Ch'an paintings are so convincingly the product of an instantaneous flash of inspiration or so perfectly illustrate the way the Ch'an painter can register his visions in terms of ink splashes.[23]" The spacing is perfect, the balance masterly, the suggestion of form, colour and texture is uncanny. As Meredith said "Perfect simplicity is unconsciously audacious." Each stalk and leaf has its subtle difference and yet all are interrelated in a way which directs the eye and unifies the composition. The ink shades build up in power towards the centre which is the focus of its calm spirit; the rest of the fruits seem to point towards this central dark shape. A still atmosphere of meditation surrounds these forms as if they were human beings. The author once stood before this painting and tried to explain its subtle qualities to another westerner who could see nothing in it. This was the nearest he ever reached towards understanding the enlightenment at which the *Ch'an* faith aimed. The difference was that the *Ch'an* master would not have tried to explain the meaning of the work. He would have remained silent.

Another field in which the *Ch'an* painters were particularly adept was in imaginary portraits of outstanding personalities, generally former worthies of their sect such as the various patriarchs. Liang K'ai, active about the same time as Mu Ch'i, only adopted the *Ch'an* modes comparatively late in life when he lived in the same monastery as Mu Ch'i. His work has a more studied quality than that of Mu Ch'i and a more conscious feeling for the virtuosity which brushwork can reveal.

Much of Liang K'ai's work has as stacatto effect produced by nervous, jagged brushwork used to depict tense figures engaged in some furious, shocking occupation like tearing up "worthless" sutras. Where Mu Ch'i is calm and contemplative, suggesting rather than stating, Liang K'ai stresses the more positive and active aspects of *Ch'an*.

MA YÜAN (ACTIVE ABOUT 1190-1230) – LANDSCAPE WITH WILLOWS – INK ON SILK (H. 9 3/8″ W. 10″) – BOSTON, MUSEUM OF FINE ARTS

A painting attributed to Liang K'ai (Plate 85) has much of the dash which we expect of his brush. It is of an immortal, a man who has cast off all wordly considerations and cares nothing for his appearance or for the criticisms of other men. A ragged, unkempt figure intent on his own inner problems strides furiously forward; one almost feels the wind he creates. The lines of the figure are dissolved into ink washes but without the slightest loss of definition or incisiveness. The variations in ink tones and the speed of the brush give this painting its spontaneity and its life. The choice of subject

87

reflects the artist's rejection of all convention and his own desire to approach the problems of representation in a completely subjective manner. In the hands of lesser masters this popular style of painting sometimes degenerated into little more than exhibitionism. And it was a style which greatly attracted later painters. In Japan, Liang K'ai's talents were recognised early and his influence has been very great. As a consequence many works, which have little chance of being by the master, carry his signature. His real œuvre preserves its freshness and vitality—the genuine eccentricity which caused the painter to be known as "Crazy Liang." In such monochrome paintings one appreciates the individualism of the Sung artists and their art which "not only demanded the highest degree of concentration and of skill in the handling of the brush, and was not only a form of painting that spurred the artist's dexterity as well as his faculty of observation; it was in its last degree and to those who had full command of it, a revelation in itself.[24]"

Two great names dominate the period from the end of the 12th to the beginning of the 13th century. This was the period when the Southern Sung Academy centred at Hangchou was enjoying its most prosperous era. Ma Yüan (active *ca.* 1190-1224) and Hsia Kuei (active *ca.* 1180-1230) were both academy painters and highly honoured by the court. Their styles have a great deal in common. Both owed much to the work of Li T'ang (*ca.* 1050-1130) (see frontispiece) whose work spanned the Northern and Southern Sung styles. Together they formed what became known as the Ma-Hsia School and their styles, easily imitated in their externals, were repeated by lesser artists down the centuries with gradual loss of power.

In the work of these two men the austerity of Li T'ang's work was replaced by refined brushwork and increased poetic sensibility. Much remains of the old orthodox styles but they are here simplified. The minute detail has been omitted and the basic framework strengthened by giving more power to the basic elements of the composition. In the increased lyricism of these landscapes, man became more important. The spectator is induced not so much to observe objectively the glories of nature as seen by the artist as to enter into and share the emotions of the figures which inhabit them. It is a more personal approach, an irresistible combination of restraint and romanticism, the clearest pictorial illustration of the universal drama of man seeking escape from his environment. Here is a theme calculated to trap the sentimentalist and later Chinese painters have been fatally tempted to imitate these two masters. They generally omitted the serenity which lies behind the inspiration of Ma Yüan and Hsia Kuei.

The compositions of this school are quite new. Instead of a carefully balanced landscape with no undue emphasis on one particular section, the landscapes of Ma Yüan in particular are deliberately selective, with the main emphasis placed in one corner so that the empty space in the other gains significance by comparison. These artists became known as "The Painters of One Corner." Together with the decorative academic styles their work has largely shaped the western idea of the whole of Chinese painting.

An outstanding example of Ma Yüan's lyrical but severe style is a fan painting *Landscape with Willows* (Plate 87). A tiny figure approaches a frail bridge between two bare willow trees, his destination being the few huts almost obscured by the mist on the far side of the river. Mountains rise in the background, their dark peaks appearing above the haze. All the main lines of the composition follow the diagonal from bottom right to top left-hand corners. By the subtlest hints we have in this small segment of nature the unmistakable impression of a broad expanse of continuing landscape. What Sirén says of another painting by Ma Yüan is equally true of this "The figure is here, as in so many of Ma Yüan's pictures, the epitome of the whole motif, representing,

HSIA KUEI (ACTIVE ABOUT 1180-1230) – A DISTANT CLEAR VIEW OF MOUNTAINS AND STREAMS – DETAIL OF A LONG SCROLL – INK ON PAPER – FORMOSA, NATIONAL GOVERNMENT COLLECTION

as it were, the mind of the painter from which the vision is reflected... the artist suggests infinity not only by utilising empty space as a potent factor in the composition, but also as a reflection in the soul of man...   There may have been greater painters in China, but no one who with a few strokes of the brush transformed shapes of nature more completely into symbols of unseen reality.[25]"

Although historians always link with Ma Yüan the name of his contemporary Hsia Kuei, and their methods have much in common, their personalities differ.  Hsia Kuei is less lyrical.  In comparison Ma Yüan seems almost a sentimentalist.  Hsia belonged to the Academy and received the Emperor's highest honour—that of the Golden Girdle.  His art owes much to Li T'ang, Fan K'uan and Mi Fei but it is abbreviated and simplified.  Plate 89 is taken from what is considered his greatest masterpiece, *A Distant Clear View of Moutains and Streams* in the National collection, Formosa.  This is a long scroll of which it is possible here only to show a fragment.  By cutting it, one destroys it but the sacrifice is inevitable for the original is over 27 feet long.  The spectator is led through a fascinating landscape of hills and valleys, rocks and

CH'ÊN JUNG (MIDDLE OF XIIIth CENTURY)
THE NINE DRAGONS (1244)
DETAIL OF A LONG SCROLL (H. 18 1/8". W. 175") – BOSTON, MUSEUM OF FINE ARTS

streams, he stops at a temple, takes a sailing boat to cross a broad lake, and as in the scene illustrated, trusts himself to a bamboo bridge. He is swept along by the power and decision of Hsia Kuei's distinctive "axe stroke" brushwork. It would be impossible to find a single weak brushstroke in the whole of its length. The brushwork is terse, the ink dense and rich; everything is sacrificed to express the boldness of these two constituents. Wheareas Ma Yüan softly suggests what is not expressed in his landscape, Hsia Kuei almost ruthlessly dissects the landscape, discarding all which detracts from the essentials. More perhaps than any other Chinese landscape scroll, it is in the full sense a majestic musical composition, the work of a Beethoven with its strong rhythms and bold themes all clearly stated and effortlessly joined. Even the atmosphere is clear and unobscured. In the hands of his many imitators this emphasis on brushwork led to exercises in a comparatively straight-forward technique but the spirit behind it was lost. Hsia Kuei, the creator of the style, held both in balance. The features of landscape, are not dissolved completely out of all reality. In the 17th century Tung Ch'i-ch'ang ended his praise of Hsia Kuei by saying "Other men work away at angles to make forms round, but this man chisels the round to make it angular."

There can be few people have not seen a Chinese dragon represented somewhere. No motif is more intimately associated with China in the popular mind than this fabulous beast. The Chinese have built a vast store of myths and legends about the animal. Reverence for it stretches back into high antiquity—to the legendary ancestors of the Chinese race. The Chinese regard it with a mixture of awe and affection. Battles in the clouds between male and female dragons are said to produce the rain and hence it has become the symbol of fertility. It is the chief of the spiritual animals of which the others are the phœnix, the unicorn and the tortoise. Dragons are believed to appear at momentous times in the history of China. Indeed, belief in the dragon has become involved with every stream of Chinese thought including Taoism and Buddhism. Finally, from its omnipotence, the dragon has become the symbol of Imperial power. In brief, it is associated with the essence of all things. "The dragon's many-sidedness as an emblem is clear from the idea that it also embodies both the male and female principle, is a symbol of utmost attainment and the embodiment of wisdom. The continuous changes and variations of life are symbolised by its unlimited powers of adaption, accomodating itself to all surroundings, therefore never finished, like the everlasting cycles of life.[26]" In art it is generally shown as a scaly reptile, the very epitome of restless energy and it is generally associated with the waters and clouds which are its proper elements.

Ch'ên Jung who lived in the 13th century was not the first but is certainly the most famous painter to be inspired by dragons and he specialised in them. His scroll *The Nine Dragons*, of which a detail is here reproduced (Plate 90), is his finest surviving work and the very essence of that ceaseless movement which characterises them. The writhing, prickly monsters sweep from the depths of the sea to the swirling clouds above, but despite their terrifying aspects, they remain strangely friendly. We too are swept along by the smooth tides of wave and vapour and feel how irrepressibly they seem to burst from the paper. Every technique in ink painting is effectively used—line, hook, splashes—and the spectator is submerged beneath an uncontrollable tide of movement and energy.

# THE
# YÜAN DYNASTY
## 1260 - 1368

THE Mongol invasion marked the climax of the constant threats to China from the less favoured tribes beyond the Great Wall. Genghiz Khan ( ? 1162-1227) spent the first part of his life till 1206 in welding the Mongol tribes into an irresistible force which, under his dynamic leadership, swept through Asia leaving a train of massacre and desolation. The highly mobile Mongol cavalry surprised and overwhelmed their enemies as effectively as the German Panzer divisions in the early stages of the last war. Had it not been for quarrels within the Mongol ruling family, they might have overrun Europe as easily as they did the eastern half of the known world. As it was, they stopped at Hungary and Poland. In 1210 the Chin empire, caught between the Mongols in the North and the opportunist Chinese in the South, was defeated and Peking burnt. Returning from campaigns in Asia in 1224, Genghiz wiped out all remaining opposition in the North and reduced the area virtually to a desert, so that it never completely recovered. Sung China then lay open to the Mongol armies.

Kublai Khan, the grandson of Genghiz and his successor, began to invade Sung China in 1235 and adopted the Imperial title in 1260—thus beginning the Mongol, or, to give it its Chinese name, the Yüan dynasty. The last Sung pretender was destroyed in 1279. Fortunately for the arts of China, the Mongols by this time had learned that a servile Chinese population was of greater value alive, with all the benefits which their craftsmen could provide, than dead. For the usual treatment meted out by the Mongols to enemies who resisted them was total annihilation.

Historians are generally hard on the Mongols and in many respects their strictures are justified. But, apart from all the seemingly wilful destruction, the Mongol regime brought some benefits. Through the safe communications which the Mongols established under the *Pax Tartarica*, Europe and China were drawn closer together and a two-way trade began. Westerners such as William of Rubruc, the envoy of St. Louis of France, were welcomed in China and the Mongols were willing to employ as administrators capable westerners who could survive the journey. The most notable was, of course, Marco Polo who served Kublai from 1275 to 1292.

93

Despite the shortness of the Mongol control of China, by official reckoning only eighty-eight years, the period left a permanent mark on Chinese painting. Much that was valuable in China was swept away, but in some of the arts, especially that of painting, the old traditions were strong enough to weather the storm and even to flower in new ways. The absence of official direction and the breakdown of schools gave individual artists freer scope to develop their own styles. Rather than serve the northern rulers, many intellectuals, from whose ranks came the artists, prefered to retire and devote themselves to the arts. Apart from one or two notable artists like Chao Mêng-fu, the Mongols managed to induce comparatively few to serve them. Their attitude to the arts in general is unknown and since painting is the most idiosyncratic of Chinese arts, they seem to have left the painters free from official interference or control.

In times of misfortune, the Chinese tend to dwell nostalgically on periods when China was independent and prosperous. Thus the major artists of the Mongol period tended to look back either to the T'ang dynasty or to the works of painters like Tung Yüan and Chü-jan whose work was so important in the 10th century. They may well have felt an affinity with them for the troubles of the Yüan period must have resembled those of the Five Dynasties. Along with this conservative tendency went an increased interest in technique and a closer study of the inter-relationship of painting and calligraphy. Painting

94

throughout the period became more a purely personal pursuit, with spiritual over-
tones, of the intellectuals, and thus there emerged the foundations of the *wên-
jên* painting, the painting of the literati or men of culture which was to influence
the development of the art in China and Japan for the following seven centuries.

The return to the T'ang showed itself in paintings of horses and in some
skilfully executed bird and flower paintings which were highly coloured and
worked out in meticulous detail; the 10th century styles reappear in fully
detailed landscapes in which the whole picture is filled with brushwork. The
lyrical Southern Sung style as seen at its most developed in the work of Ma
Yüan and Hsia Kuei, seems to have lost favour, its place being taken by heroic
landscape. A new technical facility reveals itself in a close study of earlier styles
that enabled competent artists to work in a number of different modes.

Ch'ien Hsüan (1235-1290) was the most eminent painter of flowers and
birds whose work has come down to us from the Yüan period. His life spanned
the last disturbed years of the Southern Sung and the advent of the Mongols.
He refused to serve the new masters of China and his work is obviously in the
line of bird and flower painting started in the T'ang and developed to its ultimate
degree of refinement in the academies of the Sung. Plate 94-95 shows the famous
scroll of *Insects and Lotus* in the Detroit Institute of Arts, which has become
known as *Early Autumn.*

In this painting Ch'ien Hsüan has sensitively combined a meticulous observation of some of nature's smallest creatures with a deep appreciation of the vitality which pervades their world. The scene is a composite one of his own imagination; the artist has identified himself with the insect world as if in an attempt to escape from the unpleasantness around him. A few dragonflies, grasshoppers, bees and butterflies hover over the still water in the heat of a late summer afternoon, their wings translucent in the soft light. As if to balance their light ethereal quality, a profusion of heavy overgrown water-plants in the foreground are dragged down by their own water-logged weight. The living energy and quick movement of the insects, and the intensity of the frog whose eyes are greedily fixed on a dragonfly, is offset by the listlessness of the decaying leaves. An atmosphere of misty heat rises from the water.

Other paintings by Ch'ien Hsüan show him continuing the idealistic flower and bird styles of the Sung Academy. However, in *Early Autumn* the mood is more real and atmospheric; he seems to be trying to evolve something new from the academy styles which seemed inappropriate to a ruthless period. One might summarise the difference between this and the common run of academic paintings by saying that it is painted from the inside rather than from the outside. Its genius lies not only in the organisation that results in what looks a very simple composition—but even more in a complete absence of timidity in dealing with such delicate themes. Every creature is painted with affection and sympathy; they share the same rich life as the artist, their habits and destiny correspond to his own. We have seen that the basic concept of Chinese philosophy is that man is only one of the manifestations of nature, and that harmony should exist between all things. It was never more intimately expressed than by Ch'ien Hsüan in this picture.

Since so much of the subsequent landscape painting of China springs from the Yüan masters, it is important to attempt an estimate of their work. The oldest of these, Kao K'o-kung (1248-1310) is perhaps the most difficult to assess since hardly any of his paintings have survived. His background and life is of some significance. His family came from Central Asia and he was one of the few great painters who accepted high office under Kublai. He lived much of his life in the beautiful lake-side city of Hangchou which has always inspired Chinese poets and painters by its soft, warm beauty. In typical Yüan fashion he admired Mi Fei and Li Ch'êng, Tung Yüan and Chü-jan from whom Yüan landscapes derived. He was a true *wên-jên* painter working purely for the spiritual pleasure which landscape gave him, painstakingly building up a style free from external dictation and seeking appreciation only from a small circle of cultivated people.

The landscape *Mist in Wooded Mountains* in plate 97 is dated 1333 but

96

元統癸酉夏六月
克恭

也之澤□復柳根明稠稀石峯
須溪林崇屋依敬見在生石
村高勝政
某百廿三千秋七月楚望命記

深溶那羅
莊畫與林
春伍嚴寵
柚向奇河漁
父椿舟畔
不覺義衰
重幾詐

尚題 □ □

岐居緣□却過年中苏州
人意駐紀三百年餘蓮茶
在个人辟作歲試試
成化辛卯畫廢譜今長州院

ATTRIBUTED TO KAO K'O-KUNG
(1248-1310) – MIST IN WOODED
MOUNTAINS – INK AND COLOUR ON
PAPER (H. 62 1/4". W. 29 3/4") –
FORMOSA, NATIONAL GOVERNMENT
COLLECTION

NI TSAN (1301-1374) – LANDSCAPE – DATED 1362 – INK ON PAPER (H. 11 13/16″. W. 19 13/16″) – WASHINGTON, FREER GALLERY

since, according to some authorities, he died in 1310 it can hardly be from his hand. It is, therefore, in all probability a somewhat later copy. Nevertheless, this beautiful painting must be very close to Kao K'o-kung's style in which the whole picture is filled with a highly integrated mass of detail. The brushwork is deliberately obscured and softened by colour washes to increase the effect of the mists which roll across the mountain slopes. The mists themselves are sharply defined. The technique for the peaks, though inherited from Mi Fei's dots, is more naturalistic. The two planes—foreground and background —are sharply distinguished.

Although the tenth century masters inspired Kao K'o-kung, the spirit which animates the picture is very different from that of the earlier landscapists. The earlier landscape painters strove to express the fundamental reality which lay behind the myriad externals of nature and they never allowed any sentimentality to intrude into their work. They aimed at truth expressed in brushwork of the utmost clarity. The Yüan artists are more concerned with conveying a sensation. Their landscapes are more human and more inviting.

They are dramatic but in a less overpowering way. This approach created the popular imagery of Chinese landscape painting. The use of colour itself, as a means to heighten the emotional effect of a painting and to increase its reality, has immediately softened the austere standards of the Northern Sung. The painter is no longer overawed by nature as in the 10th century, nor in love with it like the Ma-Hsia school. And one feels that he draws the emotions inspiring his pictures less from an experience of the realities of nature than from certain canons of "beauty" to which nature is made to conform. During the 16th and 17th centuries this attitude struck deep root in China and gave rise to an academic artificiality that threatened the whole future of painting.

In addition to Kao K'o-kung the landscape painting of the Yüan dynasty is dominated by four other outstanding masters, Huang Kung-wang (1269-1354), Wang Mêng (died 1385), Wu Chên (1280-*ca*. 1354) and Ni Tsan (1301-1374). They are collectively known as "The Four Great Masters of the Yüan Dynasty" and their styles greatly influenced subsequent scholar painters who took them as their ideal.

The work of Ni Tsan, the last of the Four Great Masters, is the most distinctive of the group. Its apparent simplicity and extreme economy of means, however, belie the rigid discipline behind it. It is this unobtrusive power which in Chinese thought gives a picture dignity[27]. His style, like that of Mi Fei, was copied and imitated over the centuries and work "Inspired by Ni Tsan" "In the style of Ni Tsan" or just optimistically signed "Ni Tsan," exist in their hundreds. Few of his imitators succeeded in combining the restrained power of his brush and the purity of his spirit. Plate 98 is typical of his style and of a number of compositions by him. The ink is very dry and used most sparingly, "like gold" say the Chinese. The pale tones are modulated very subtly. Even the white paper seems to have its very special tonal value. Heavy dots are used only very occasionally to give the impression of vegetation growing on his rocks or up the mountain slopes. A few lean trees and a low, broad-roofed hut occupy the foreground, the middle distance is glossed over by a broad expanse of calm water which leads into a range of flat mountains in the background. The trees on their arid foreshore seem to find life as difficult as it must have been for the sensitive man during the last unhappy decades of the Mongols. The rocks are sharply cut but never tortured. Human beings find no place in his quiet world.

One recognises in this work a fastidious and independent mind. He was the ideal scholar-painter, the philosopher who could discard all worldly possessions and reject a world whose passions and brutalities offended him. He could devote himself to travel, give his paintings to those he felt appreciated them even if they were humble peasants, who could seek in communion with nature the standards which alone contented him. One sees his landscapes through the soft, grey lens of a morning mist when the light is evenly distributed over the countryside. He shrinks from expression of all violence of weather and landscape feature—a silent spirit in a still world. His range is small, his technique limited but within strictly chosen limits, impeccable. Of all Chinese landscapits he is the most reticent, delicate and refined. The genius of his work is most difficult to assess for he says more with a few strokes than any artist after him. It is the essence of purity and deliberation.

The last Yüan painting here reproduced is *Feeding Horses* by the 14th century artist Jên Jên-fa. We know little about him apart from the fact that he came from the south of China and, towards the end of the Yüan dynasty, reached high office in the service of the Mongols. He made his name as a painter of horses but Buddhist paintings, landscapes and street scenes by him have also survived, mostly in Japan. This small painting in the Victoria and Albert Museum is perhaps the best of a number of paintings of horses attributed to him; it is certainly the liveliest, most sensitive and most original. In a simple scene, he has calmly observed and carefully balanced a group of horses and men, expressing a relationship between them which is new in this type of painting. He shows himself to be a master with a complete technique; foreshortening and overlapping, light and shade present no difficulties.

The Mongols understood little of most aspects of Chinese culture in general and painting in particular, but they shared with the Chinese a love of horses. As we have seen, horses were a popular subject for painting from at least the early T'ang period and it is understandable that the Chinese, who were hoping at least to educate their masters, should try to appeal to them through this particular aspect of their art. The most famous Yüan painter of horses was Chao Mêng-fu (1254-1322) who also served the foreign rulers. He painted some scrolls of energetic horses exercising in landscape. Jên Jên-fa who was probably a contemporary of Chao worked in a more refined manner and his draughtsmanship is more sensitive than that of his better known contemporary. The grooms are well characterised and the whole scene is highly atmospheric—the impression of light seems to suggest the early morning.

Some aspects of Jên's work compare with that of the 11th century master Li Lung-mien who painted a famous scroll of horses. However, this composition tries to make a break with the tradition of long scrolls which, through constant repetition, tended to monotony. Han Kan is a better comparison, for one must not forget that, during this period of national humiliation, a Chinese like Jên Jên-fa would rather seek consolation and inspiration in the most venerable traditions of the great T'ang age than in the more recent Sung. This was their subtle method of implying criticism. The world of Jên Jên-fa was no

100

JEN JEN-FA (ACTIVE IN THE XIVth CENTURY) – FEEDING HORSES – INK AND SLIGHT COLOUR ON SILK (H. 21 5/8″. W .30″) –
LONDON, VICTORIA AND ALBERT MUSEUM

doubt brutal and hard but here, at least, is a painter whose spirit remained unbroken. The vigour, naturalism and attention to detail of this late Yüan painting seem to presage the painting of the early Ming period.

After the death of Kublai, in 1294, the Chinese empire of the Mongols rapidly disintegrated. Most of his successors only occupied the throne for a very short time and had neither his authority nor the backing of a united Mongol Asia to support them. Their empire began to split up into a number of independent kingdoms under the various members of the Mongol ruling family. The tide of economic and political unrest in China steadily mounted. Famine and the debasement of the currency reduced the country to a system of barter. Rumours that the Mongols intended to put down the opposition in the country

101

by such fanatic brutality as killing all Chinese with certain very common surnames played into the hands of the secret societies which China has always produced in times of discontent. Their vile laws, venal administration, terror and above all the economic distress caused by inflation, exploitation of the farming population and agrarian breakdown brought the country to a state of desperation which Kublai's less effective successors could not control. As always, it took some years for a leader of sufficient strength to appear who could unite the various factions into a force capable of sweeping away the remains of the faded Mongol power.

As in the time of the Han, it was a man of low birth who achieved this. Chu Yüan-chang, a monk turned soldier, made himself master of the Yangtze river and, in 1368, he drove the last Mongol ruler out of China back to the northern areas. Though troublesome, they were never again to provide a serious threat to the new dynasty—the Ming or "brilliant" as it was named when Chu had himself proclaimed its First Emperor in 1368. China was once again under a native ruling house.

THE Ming dynasty made a promising start by destroying the hated Mongols and putting in their place a purely Chinese ruling house. As well as restoring Chinese confidence and self-esteem, the new rulers brought a much-needed peace and rapid economic recovery to a disrupted and bankrupt country. The first emperors tried sincerely to interest the powerful scholar-official class and to revive and preserve the achievements of Chinese culture. They restored many of the cultural offices of the Sung and supported such projects as vast encyclopaedias which created a good impression among the intelligensia. The army was very efficiently reorganised and Chinese arms, though never as powerful as in T'ang times, were paramount for a century or so throughout the east. In a burst of reconstructive effort the new dynasty rebuilt the ruined cities of China. Nanking, the first Ming capital, has fundamentally changed little from the city as Chu Yüan-chang, the founder of the Ming, laid it out. The popular arts of the drama and the novel flourished, contributing greatly to Chinese literary wealth, though the scholarly mind has only come to accept their importance during the last century. At the top of the social scale, the sybaritic life of the Ming upper classes encouraged the decorative arts—especially those of ceramics, lacquer and metalwork. Architecture became a great preoccupation of this reconstructing dynasty : the beautiful cities of Hangchou and Suchou developed into great centres of intellectual life where men of taste and culture gathered to discuss the arts, and where the accomplishments of calligraphy, painting, chess or gambling "brought men together in a community of pleasure". Here wealthy scholars formed huge libraries and great collections of works of art. In contrast with the scantiness of the remains of Sung painting there is no lack of Ming work.

However, historians both eastern and western have often decried the achievements of the Ming centuries. Except in craftworks, the dynasty is generally condemned for being "commonplace". It is true that in most things the new dynasty looked back to the T'ang and professed its loyalty only to already conventional ideals. It was frankly conservative and obsessed by the fear of any change which might be incompatible with the ordered peace it strove to maintain. New ways of thought were strongly discouraged. Confucianism as interpreted by the Sung philosophers became the pillar of the state and any candidate for position in the civil service who strayed from the orthodox interpretations in his examination papers had little hope of success. The result was that many of the most important artists of the period either stayed outside the administration or served for a very short time, whilst all traditional painting was overwhelmed by a wave of pedantry. A shrinking horror of vulgarity inhibited the more original minds.

The arts of poetry and painting, traditionally the main interest of educated Chinese, had flowered during the T'ang and Sung periods. Many scholars of the Ming contented themselves with elaborating, refining, and exploiting in detail the attitudes of the earlier creative epochs. No artist of sufficient genius arose during the 15th century to contribute anything radically new to these two greatest of Chinese arts. The Buddhist faith, even Ch'an, which had inspired sculptors and painters for nearly a millenium was losing its power to stimulate. Any expression of a deep emotion in art seems to have been at a discount. Perhaps the greatest activity was in the twin fields of collecting and connoisseurship—activities which by their very nature look backwards. In a real sense the Chinese were for a while stifled by their own achievements. Only the most revolutionary artists in the 16th century managed to free themselves from the weight of their cultural heritage.

Perhaps even more significant for the development of Chinese painting is the inherent Chinese tendency to study and to perfect. Once an art form was introduced the Chinese rapidly mastered and perfected it—often destroying its vigour in the process. When painting became the prerogative of the scholar it was bound to lose much of its spontaneity and become antiquarian in bias. The scholar artists of the Ming devoted themselves to a painstaking analysis of the rich innovations of the masters of the Five Dynasties, Sung and Yüan and gained great satisfaction from their ability to paint in the styles of the earlier masters. With originality at such a discount it is hardly surprising that more than a thousand Ming artists have been recorded. Brushstrokes, compositions, subjects and colours were minutely considered, reduced to their essentials and classified. Treatises on these subjects aimed at putting painting techniques at the disposal of everyman. At the end of the dynasty, in 1633, a book of wood-block illustrations entitled *The Collected Painting of the Ten Bamboo Hall* appeared. This was the first of many such pattern books which, while popularizing the art, threatened to destroy all originality of thought.[28]

From this time the distinction between professional and amateur painters became more sharply drawn. The professional painters included those who lived by their art, holding positions in academies and at court. Amateur artists gained no financial reward from their painting; for them it was an indispensible intellectual pursuit of a cultured life. They ranged from some of the most important artists of the period down to the hundreds of petty officials who dabbled in the art. Some were genuine artists, others had no more claim to being called artists than the myriad young ladies of the 19th century who "took views of Rome" in their sketchbooks. But because the connoisseurs and writers on painting were all scholars and amateur painters, their criticisms of the professionals were ungenerous in the extreme.

The opening years of the Ming dynasty were dominated by a number of very competent masters who had weathered the troubled years which saw the collapse of the Yüan rulers and the establishment of the Ming. As is to be expected, in landscape, the styles so completely developed by the Four Great Masters were paramount.

But, if the first half of the Ming period was one in which the achievements of past centuries were being digested, they were also being clarified. This can be seen if we turn away from landscape to another great field of Chinese painting—bamboo.

The bamboo plant holds a unique place in the affections of the Chinese in general and in their painting in particular. The attentions which the West lavishes on the rose, to take the most obvious parallel, are as nothing to the care with which the Chinese, and to a lesser degree, the Japanese grow and study the bamboo. A whole cult has grown up around it, with a wide range of symbolic references. It is pliant but unbreakable, thereby combining two attributes of the gentleman as specified by Confucius. It is often referred to in Chinese inscriptions as "This gentleman". It withstands the winter cold and is flattered by such names as "green jade"—thereby being equated with the most precious material known to eastern civilisation. "Even when the snow is ten feet deep, how should they bow their heads?" says a Chinese poet. No home, especially that of a scholar, would be considered worthy if it was not graced with some bamboos. Thus we read many a lament from a Chinese scholar in a distant province that he cannot make the bamboos grow. The various species were closely studied, and their peculiar virtues described in detail. Innumerable poems and paintings express their every mood—bamboos in the wind, in the rain, in the mist, by day, by night, by the riverside, in the mountains: a few leaves, a dense thicket. Some painters devoted their whole lives to depicting this plant alone.

Technically they provide an ideal subject for the spontaneous monochrome ink painting which is the glory of Chinese art. They demand an intelligent assimilation by the artists and an unhesitating, faultless execution. In a bamboo painting the least fault, or hesitancy of the brush, destroys the organic quality of the plant.

Literary records suggest that bamboo painting started as early as the T'ang dynasty but it was not until the early Sung that it became a major passion and the object of specialisation. Most Chinese painters from the Sung dynasty onwards profess admiration for the 11th century painter Wên T'ung who specialised in the subject. He seems to have established the standards which most later artists tried to emulate. Su Tung-p'o, a friend and student of Wên T'ung transmitted his master's instructions on bamboo. "Painters of today draw joint after joint and pile up leaf on leaf. How can that become a bamboo ? When you are going to paint a bamboo you must first realise the thing completely in your mind. Then grasp the brush, fix your attention, so that you see clearly what you wish to paint : start quickly, move the brush, follow straight what you see before you, as the buzzard swoops down when the hare jumps out. If you hesitate one moment, it is gone.[29]" Over the years bamboo became the

106

test of the gentleman painter, the mirror of his own character, the touchstone of his penetration of the mysteries of nature, the infallible mirror of his calligraphic skill with the brush.

The literature on Chinese painting has, since at least Ming times, been bedevilled by two terms which must here be explained. The first is *wên-jên-hua* and the second *nan-tsung-hua*. The distinctions which they try to make continued into the 19th century. They are often either artificial or completely invalid but as products of the Ming dynasty writers one must understand them in considering the painting of this period.

*Wên-jên-hua* means "painting by literary men". Fundamentally this denotes the art produced by amateurs as distinct from professionals. Historians trace the distinction back to the first centuries A.D. when scholars took to painting as a pastime and as a means of expressing their most exalted thoughts. In fact, the classification rests on social rather than on artistic grounds. But during the late T'ang and Sung dynasties it came to have a stylistic reference. The professional painters who entered the Imperial Academies tended to paint in a naturalistic manner with a close adherence to outline. The works of Hui-tsung (Plate 73) are typical of the Academic approach. The literary men, on the other hand, used much freer modes and naturalism was anathema to them. Their view of nature was more emotional and idealistic and their techniques more "impressionistic". There was, however, much inter-relationship between the two modes. During the Ming period, the emperors, in their determination to preserve the past and follow strictly orthodox lines, kept the noses of their professional court painters very firmly to the academic grindstone. Thus their work became highly conventional and originality was virtually extinguished. The main effort of the Court group of professional painters was in the direction of formalism and technical proficiency. These men dominated the first half of the period.

The amateur painters, however, true to their traditional attitude, revolted from the dry manners and lifeless work of the professionals and generally followed what was called the *nan-tsung-hua* or Southern School Painting, so that in a sense the field of reference of this term overlaps that of *wên-jên-hua*.

The term *nan-tsung-hua* describes a mode in opposition to the *pei-tsung-hua* "Northern School Painting". Both terms exclusively concern landscape painting. They were evolved by the late Ming theorists Mo Shih-lung (active *ca.* 1567-1582) and Tung Ch'i-ch'ang (1555-1636) and based on an analogy with the split in Buddhism which took place in the T'ang dynasty. The "Northern School" style described works which were in the academic tradition of Ma Yüan and Hsia Kuei (Plates 87 and 89) and in that of their successors, the Chê School (see later in this chapter). Their tendency was to stress colour, outline and detail in a manner which goes back to Li Ssu-hsün of the T'ang. The term "Southern School" paintings however, indicates works in the softer, more atmospheric monochrome styles of the literary men, particularly Mi Fei (Plate 71) and the Four Great Masters of the Yüan Dynasty. The T'ang dynasty painter Wang Wei was the spiritual founder of the School. Northern and Southern, in this connotation have no geographic significance. During the Ming and Ch'ing dynasties, most amateur gentleman painters used the Southern School styles, and based themselves mainly on the work of the Four Great Masters (see plate 98). From the point of view of composition, the Northern style landscapes followed the Ma Yüan-Hsia Kuei lyrical manner which concentrated on only one corner of the scene leaving a great deal blank to be filled by the imagination of the spectator. The Southern School turned away from this approach which had become weakened and sentimentalised, and had been worked to death. They cultivated the broad, comprehensive views of landscape which appear at their best in the work of the Four Great Masters of the Yüan. Technically speaking, they placed increased emphasis on line. Instead of the soft washes used for mountains, the amateur painters made a close study of the methods whereby they could denote landscape features by series of small lines. Practice in doing this gave every man who could write and was prepared to master a basic repertoire of strokes, the ability to paint. Needless to say the proportion of true artists remained small.

Another trend of significance for the history of China became more evident during the Ming period. This was the increasing political and economic cleavage between the north and south of the country. By this time the main centres of intellectual activity had been firmly established in the south. Over the course of several centuries most of the older families had taken refuge in the comparative safety of the south far removed from the frequent invasions by the tribes in the lands bordering China's northern frontier. Peking, the traditional capital, was actually unsuited to serve as a national centre. Geographically it was vulnerable to northern invaders, the population of the surrounding regions was much less than that of the south and communications were difficult. However, the examination system decreed that candidates should be selected on a strictly regional basis. The administration remained the only legitimate employment for men of culture but the one third of China containing Peking thus supplied as many officials as the very much more populous and intellectually active areas in the south. The result was that, once the Ming had moved the capital back to Peking, many scholars in the densely populated south failed to obtain the positions which their talents merited. On one hand, this led to dissatisfaction which found expression in political unrest. On the other, it meant that many men turned to the arts. As will be explained later, this completely undermined the traditional conception of the amateur painter. Since unemployed scholars were often only too glad to be able to support themselves by selling their paintings, the distinction between professional and amateur became even more unreal.

About a half century passed before the official style of the Ming period began to take shape. During the reign of Hsüan-tê (1426-1435) who was an emperor with artistic pretentions, a number of capable painters gathered at the court. Of these Tai Chin (active 1430-1455) was the most adept and exercised the greatest influence on his successors. Chinese historians forgive his professionalism, possibly because he gained little financial reward from his services to the court. Perhaps he could not bear its stifling atmosphere for he stayed there for only a brief period and then retired to his native Hangchou in Chekiang where he spent the rest of his life as a painter. He died in poverty. Many artists followed his style and he is considered the founder of the Chê School so named after the first character in the name Chekiang.

109

LÜ CHI (ACTIVE CIRCA 1500) – GRASS,
FLOWERS AND WILD BIRDS – INK AND COLOUR
ON PAPER (H. 75 3/4″. W. 33 3/4″) –
FORMOSA, NATIONAL GOVERNMENT COLLEC-
TION

Plate 106 and 107 is taken from a long scroll *Life on the River*. The decisive brushwork immediately recalls the distinctive Ma Yüan-Hsia Kuei style of the Southern Sung Academy on which he based his work. The trees, rocks, boats and figures echo the interpretations of these great lyricists. The forms he uses are accomplished and faultlessly composed: the eye is led from one centre of interest to another without a break. Fishermen steer their boats with the stream or pole them against it: some moor their craft under the trees to take a meal on the shore: others while away the waiting moments huddled in silent contemplation of the water or chat with each other under the awnings rigged over their shallow punts. The ink tones are carefully modulated to give the impression of a rich and varied riverside foliage.

The essential difference between this and the work of the earlier masters lies in a basically different interest. We are here asked to share the life of the fishermen, to envy their rustic simplicity. Tai Chin makes no demands on our innermost souls. His harmony with nature is reflected as an acute observation of the world and its inhabitants. It is an intimate personal view sensitively expressed. We are no longer awed by grandeur, or tempted to share a moment of solitary communion and hushed stillness. All is bustle and life, and we are swept along in its stream. The mystical or lyrical approach of the great Sung painters is replaced by an amused interest in the myriad facets of daily life. The painter simplifies for purposes of clarity not for those of evocation.

The general vision of Tai Chin is more dry and clear-cut than that of Ma Yüan and Hsia Kuei. The brushwork is powerful but one feels that it is a studied power, that the technique is more important than the spirit. Nevertheless, the Ming painters as a whole, in sacrificing the mystery or awe which moved earlier artists, developed a genuine love of the facts they saw before them, and every detail became the object of humble affection and close study. But it was an attitude that contained the seeds of its own destruction by making it all too easy for the multitude of lesser artists to substitute cold analysis and meticulous description.

What has become universally known as the Academic Style in Chinese painting became completely formulated during the Ming Dynasty. It is seen at its best in the prolific work of Lü Chi who was active at the court during the late 15th century. His style became the standard for later Academy painters and had many imitators. It is, perhaps unfortunately, the kind of Chinese painting which first attracted the western eye, and most museums possess a work by him, or attributed to him. He was especially popular in Japan where he strongly influenced the screen painters. Even the great Japanese master Sesshū, who went to China (*ca.* 1467) and complained that he could find there no great painters or original styles, came under the spell of Lü Chi.

*Grass, Flowers and Wild Birds* in plate 110 is a typical large decorative composition which inherited all the good qualities of the Sung Academy of Hui-tsung and inflated them to suit the grandiose spirit of the Ming court. The composition is bold, impressive and quite frankly decorative. Two pheasants search for food among some sketchily indicated boulders. A spray of wild grass sweeps in an arc through the whole picture, blown by the wind and bent beneath the weight of some smaller birds. A complete naturalism and an impeccable harmony pervades the whole work. In their own way, these nature studies illustrate as clearly as the landscapes the tendency of Ming artists to seek an ever closer, more intimate association with nature. But, it is a nature tamed and organised into a garden where men of sensibility take their ease in the comfortable contemplation of things beautiful. Nevertheless, these are not the meticulous and dead botanical studies of later painters : a vibrant life flows through them which, despite occasional sentimentality and artificiality, is always impressive. The fact that Shên Chou, one of the really outstanding amateur painters of the Ming dynasty, considered this painting worthy of his inscription shows that he felt it to be of considerable artistic merit and perhaps that it perfectly reflected one aspect of Ming taste.

SHÊN CHOU (1427-1509) – SITTING UP AT NIGHT – INK AND COLOUR ON PAPER (H. 28 1/4″. W. 9″) – FORMOSA, NATIONAL GOVERNMENT COLLECTION

As painting became increasingly an indispensible ingredient of the cultured life, the numbers of recorded painters swelled to giant proportions. Unlike earlier periods, many genuine works by the greatest masters have survived. Although a number of them were very eclectic or had their own individual styles, it is convenient to consider them under the schools into which Chinese historians have divided them.

Under Tai Chin we have already discussed the Chê School which he founded. The other school, the Wu School, was founded in Wu-hsien (modern Suchou) by Shên Chou (1427-1509), one of the most capable artists who appeared during the Ming centuries. Whereas Tai Chin is criticised for being a professional artist and cultivating the more decorative side of painting, Shên Chou was an amateur for whom landscape was a source of deep spiritual inspiration. The term "amateur" in the west suggests dilletante. This is far from being an accurate description of Shên Chou and it would be better to call him simply a "non-professional" for Shên Chou devoted his whole life to the arts with the sincerest dedication. Painting provided him with the ideal means of combining the Chinese metaphysical approach to nature with the qualities expected of a cultured life—a deep knowledge of poetry, literature and calligraphy. His life and work reflected the complete detachment from all wordly considerations which is the aim of the traditional Chinese philosophy of living.

Shên Chou was everything that an ideal *wên-jên* painter should be. The biographies sing his praises almost *ad nauseum*. He was brilliant in all the arts. His life was a model of other-wordly virtue. He devoted his life to his mother thereby satisfying the Confucian demands of filial piety. Rejecting all offers of official position, he lived a humble life almost to the extent of being a hermit. He was generous to a fault, giving his paintings to whoever he felt would appreciate them and spurning all rewards and honours. Such praises are sung of so many Chinese painters that one begins to doubt their validity, but it would seem that Shên Chou was indeed a man of genuine learning and simple heart.

As an artist his personality is clear. Historically speaking, the Wu School carried on the traditions of the Great Masters of the Yüan dynasty who in their turn took their inspiration from Tung Yüan and Chü-jan. Although he had studied all the great masters and could paint in their various styles, the influence of the Northern Sung and Yüan masters predominates. However, whereas the early masters were awed by nature and the Yüan masters fascinated by its beauty, Shên Chou and his successors were intimately concerned with man's close association with it. *Sitting up at Night* (Plate 112) is a typical reflection of this more poetic, more confident polite relationship. The warm tones of ink and colour give the landscape a soft beauty but a preoccupation with the beguiling techniques of brushwork introduce a certain dryness which only his sincerity and draughtsmanship save from monotony. He is grateful for the beauties of nature and completely master of it. He approaches nature on equal terms and forms an ideal world in which he can relax. In spirit he incorporates much of the Ma Yüan school. If we do injustice to this achievement it is because his work has been so often weakly imitated. At its best we must admire a perfect technique and a superbly cultivated spirit. Shên Chou was one of the few great artists of the Ming dynasty whose sense of the beauty of nature was not smothered by orthodoxy, but he has no fundamentally new vision.

Shên Chou's most outstanding pupil, Wên Ch'eng-ming (1470-1559), continued and refined the traditions of the Wu School. The Chinese consider him also as an ideal scholar-painter. He came of a family which had provided many officials and he, too, was destined to serve the administration. However, he never reached high office—according to some authorities because he failed his examinations—and he soon retired to spend the last thirty years of his life in the pursuit of the arts of painting, poetry and calligraphy. Certainly, amidst the delightful surroundings of Suchou and in the company of an intellectual elite, he found the life of the lofty, disinterested scholar more to his liking. Without exception the Chinese histories praise his high character and moral integrity.

The paintings he produced over a long life of nearly ninety years |vary considerably in style and depth of feeling. Critics generally agree in placing his finest and most original works in the last ten years of his life when he seems to have acquired a genuine delight in painting, and an inspiration which raised his works to the realm of great painting. A new vigour of brush and freedom of spirit inspired his later years. The main formative influence of his life was undoubtedly that of his master Shên Chou but in this vein he lacks Shên Chou's independence of spirit. He allowed himself to be influenced by the Sung and Yüan masters, especially by Li T'ang and Wu Chên, but we see echoes also of Li Lung-mien and Chao Mêng-fu. Again, much of his work recalls the delicacy and accurate draughtsmanship of T'ang Yin (see below). It is clear that for the majority of his life he was quite eclectic—a scholar and an antiquarian interpreting many styles of the past in his own meticulous manner. He felt little need for originality and was content to wander at will through China's rich past.

The painting reproduced in plate 115, *Spring in Chiang-nan* is typical of one of the best known of his styles and of much mid-Ming landscape painting. It is dated 1547 and is a characteristic scholar painting. It depends for its success on careful drawing and the sensitive use of colour. The long surface

114

is divided into three planes, the transitions between them being effected by clumps of trees. A lonely figure in a boat sits calmly contemplating the stillness and the colours of early spring. The landscape is flooded by pale light.

Wen's technique is impeccable but his is an artificial world. The intention is to evoke a poetic atmosphere of otherworldliness and purity which were the ideals of his society. If, indeed, he is attempting to paint a genuine sensation, it is a weak one. One can see the purity of spirit for which he is praised, but the restraint is so overplayed that it has become a source of weakness. This is made very clear if we compare his work with that of Shên Chou whose hermit's life gave him a more instinctive and genuine experience of landscape. In a way Wên's work can be called a scholarly attempt to fuse the T'ang coloured style with the landscape paintings of the Yüan scholars. It is the acme of aestheticism.

It is unfortunate for the historian of art that artists are such individual and changeable creatures. They do not always fit themselves into the neat categories and schools which the historian invents for his own convenience. This is particularly true of some of the most renowned painters of the mid-Ming period. For example T'ang Yin and Ch'iu Ying. These two remarkable

WÊN CH'ENG-MING (1470-1559) – SPRING IN CHIANG-NAN – DATED 1547 – INK ON PAPER (H. 51 3/8″. W. 18 3/8″). – FORMOSA, NATIONAL GOVERNMENT COLLECTION

painters, who did most to shape Ming taste, stand outside the various schools formed in these centuries. They developed one style in particular for which they are most famous. It was taken up by artisans in later centuries and introduced to the west as decoration on porcelain and lacquer. There it greatly influenced 18th century European taste. In their own country it provided a style suited to the colour print which in its turn gave the initial stimulus to the vast Japanese wood-block print movement known as *ukiyo-e*, "the pictures of the floating world." Indeed the art of T'ang Yin and Ch'iu Ying and the popular imagery they created has conditioned the conventional western concept of "Chinese painting" much to the detriment of an appreciation of the more sublime achievements of the art. The works of these two men were genuine individual achievements but they sowed seeds which almost destroyed the art of Chinese painting.

T'ang Yin (1470-1523) is one of the most popular figures in the history of Chinese art. He showed remarkable scholastic brilliance as a youth but his prospects of a successful career were ruined when, at his examinations in Peking, he was involved in a ruse to obtain foreknowledge of the questions. He returned to Suchou in disgrace and spent the rest of his life in painting, in the full enjoyment of the wine and women of his city and in travel to the beauty spots of China. Late in life he turned to Buddhism. He remained at heart a man of literary and scholarly turn of mind and mixed freely with the cultured classes. However, his conduct shocked the moral standards of the time and many prominent scholars, although they admired his work, mourned the dissipation of his genius.

His painting was in great demand—so much so that his teacher Chou Ch'ên and his pupils were pressed into service to provide works which he signed. He was very eclectic and worked in many styles—from the grand and noble manner of the early Sung landscape masters, to a free manner which foreshadows the individualists of the next two centuries. His work was often copied. It is thus very difficult in the present state of our knowledge to form a true picture of his achievements. It is not easy to place a man whose work ranges from pure *wên-jên* painting to the dryest Academy style.

We have selected for reproduction (Pl. 118) a painting in yet another style for which he was most famous. It is a figure painting essentially Ming in taste and execution. A man is seated in a garden. Behind him, as if to produce a stage which improves on nature, are some delightful landscape screens. Two ladies acompany him, one holding a white peonie. Before him is a fantastic rock and a square pot of flowers. A bough of plum blossom intruding above the screen is the only natural element in this open-air setting. The figures are graceful and naturalistic, their relationship is subtly suggested and the whole setting is the apogee of grace and refinement. They breathe the relaxed air of Suchou. The artificiality of the scene is tempered by an exquisite sense of style which has survived the hundred thousand repetitions on porcelain in subsequent ages.

The inscription refers to a book of gossip about T'ang poets and tells how a minor poet named Ts'ui Yao ruined the reputation of a courtesan by writing a scurrilous poem about her. The poor girl became quite ill and meeting the poet begged him to take pity on her, restore her good name and her popularity which he did. The picture therefore probably represents the poet and his victim.

Ch'iu Ying came from obscure parents and was fortunate to be taken under the care of T'ang Yin's teacher Chou Ch'ên. He was essentially a professional painter, a serious, prolific worker who enjoyed great popularity and patronage.

As an artist he, too, had many sides. He took elements from both the Wu and Chê Schools. He is famous for some fine copies of old masters which provide valuable evidence for old works now lost. He made illustrative pictures in colour which he filled with meticulous detail. Occasionally he used a more individual and bold ink style. He is best known for his paintings of figures in landscapes. These aim at reproducing the ideal of intellectual rusticity, the kind of gentle life which, thanks to their private fortunes, the educated classes could live amidst the beauties of Suchou. He had a complete technique at his command. His work shows the technical perfection and eclecticism which are the hall-marks of Ming art.

The painting reproduced in plate 117 is one of a pair in the National Collection, Formosa. In a refined and polished composition two gentlemen stop to chat in the shade of a tree whose leaves are touched with pale blue. Behind it rises a huge strange-shaped rock done in freer brushwork. The faces of the figures are very naturalistic, their robes a model of drapery representation for which the Chinese are famous. In work which is always a model of clarity, Ch'iu Ying harmonised the traditions of many centuries of Chinese painting and developed a style calculated to make a strong popular appeal. His work is the apogee of Ming taste—suave, accomplished and balanced. If anything it is too polite and unemotional. He produces a mood without any real depth of feeling. It is wrong to decry his work since we often judge it by its later purely decorative derivations and by the mass of copies later artisans made. In his own way he was an innovator and he stands at the end of a long line of Chinese painting which started with the coloured works of the Northern School masters in the T'ang dynasty. His work marks one climax of the Chinese domination of landscape. One might almost say that he destroys it by transforming it into an ideal garden.

117

善和坊裏李端端<br>
白牡丹花月揚州金滿市佳人<br>
價反屬窮酸唐寅

T'ANG YIN (1470-1523) – POET AND TWO COURTESANS – INK AND COLOUR ON SILK – FORMOSA, NATIONAL GOVERNMENT COLLECTION

CH'IU YING (ACTIVE CIRCA 1522-60) – CONVERSATION
UNDER A TUNG TREE – INK AND COLOUR ON PAPER
(H. 145 1/8″. W. 45 5/8″) – FORMOSA, NATIONAL
GOVERNMENT COLLECTION

An eminent Japanese scholar, Y. Yonezawa has called T'ang Yin and Ch'iu Ying "Neo-Academicians" who based their work on certain Sung Academy painters and Yüan masters. He makes the interesting point that this type of painting could only emerge in the transitional period when the amateurs were beginning to take over the leading position and become the arbiters of taste. Living in Suchou such professionals could still associate with the leading amateur literary talents of the time and take from them what they needed for their art. After their deaths its very popularity made the work of these two artists unacceptable to cultivated taste, and the neo-academic style dropped completely from the world of serious Chinese painting.

The paintings of T'ang Yin and Ch'iu Ying have an irresistible charm. They epitomise for many westerners a Chinese way of life as ideal and perfect as it was in fact limited and artifical. But the art of these two painters represented only one side of the Chinese artistic genius. It is fortunate for the history of Chinese painting that a vigorous group of revolutionaries appeared to counteract their influence. Otherwise with T'ang Yin and Ch'iu Ying the art might well have petered out.

Throughout the history of Chinese painting there seem always to have been two fundamental modes—the meticulous truth to nature of the men who generally ended in the academies and the freer, more personal modes of various artists of individual and original turn of mind. Any tendency to over-formalise painting (and this was always strong) seems immediately to produce an equally powerful reaction. The "Individualist" movement is extremely difficult to discuss adequately. Each man is his own standard and only occasionally did he have followers, almost never a school. This tradition of the movement stretches back to the earliest times and would be a valuable subject for study. The artists are generally characterised as drunkards, ne'er-do-wells, brilliant but unbalanced creatures. They work when the spirit moves them or when they have no money left for wine. The sell their paintings when necessity drives them to it, otherwise they give them away. Chinese society, in some respects the most rigid in the world, has always recognised their genius, provided them with the means to live and regarded them with great affection. The Chinese like the English have a rigid social code but also a peculiar affection for eccentric personalities.

Hsü Wei (1529-1593) is a model for this type of wayward artistic personality. He is even accused of murder and attempted suicide. He served as a minor official for a short time but hated bureaucratic life and spent most of his years in riotous living. He was extremely poor but a man of great ability in all the arts and one of the few Ming painters who worked on a higher level of

120

冬爛包蕉春一荸漏墻倦笑老梅容
世間哪事誰無濕他壓盃兒文様
殷者藤漵老墨誰

HSÜ WEI (1529-1593) –
ROCKS, BANANA AND PLUM
TREES – INK AND SLIGHT
COLOUR ON PAPER
(H. 65 3/4″. W. 35 7/8″) –
STOCKHOLM, NATIONAL
MUSEUM

imagination. He began to paint only late in life. We hear of no teacher and his work seems to break all the accepted rules of painting. It met with comparatively little recognition in his own time but became very highly appreciated after his death and had great influence on the various individualists of the next two hundred years. It is still alive in the work of some of China's most influential modern painters who have kept to the Chinese style. In the author's opinion the future of Chinese painting lay almost entirely with such men.

*Rocks, Banana and Plum Trees* (Plate 121) shows how violent was the effort required to escape from the formality of his artistic atmosphere. He takes a small fragment of nature and, using his technique like a lens, breaks it down to a few powerfully rendered basic elements. Unlike most Ming painting it is never " polite " or " good mannered ". On the contrary, one senses a deliberate attempt to shock. The power of brushwork and ink is heavily emphasised. It is important to notice that the calligraphy is as eccentric as the picture. The painter endeavours to produce a style, which is his and his alone. The classical accomplished brushwork is deliberately destroyed—almost mocked. Occasionally, as if to show his ability and contempt or to serve as a foil, he does employ the traditional strokes to depict a few bamboo leaves or twigs of plum blossom. With their speed, immediacy and almost casual approach, these painters were in fact reasserting and keeping alive the first canon of painting which Hsieh Ho laid down in the 6th century—the " reverberation of the life-breath ".


There is perhaps no other painter who has raised so many passions as Tung Ch'i-ch'ang (1555-1636). Opinions on him vary from " superb technician" and "daring master of composition" to "prejudiced bore" and "dreary imitator". Earlier historians, in their love of the painting of the Sung dynasty, condemned his austere scholastic approach. Lately critics have appraised his work more favourably. Certainly he was the ideal Ming *wên-jen* painter, the cultivated amateur for whom the art was the purest expression of the spirit.

Tung Ch'i-ch'ang was a high official and a man of broad culture, wealthy and gifted, moderate and well-balanced in his life—a man of very scholarly and antiquarian turn of mind. Ch'an Buddhism seems to have been the deepest influence on his life and it shows in the calmness of his paintings though it does not manifest itself in the sudden enlightenment and rapid execution which we saw in earlier Ch'an masters. He spent a great deal of his time in the company of like-minded scholars and artists such as Mo Shih-lung (active *ca.* 1567-1582) and Ch'ên Chi-ju (1558-1639) looking at and discussing the many fine paintings which passed through their hands. These were the men who formulated the

122

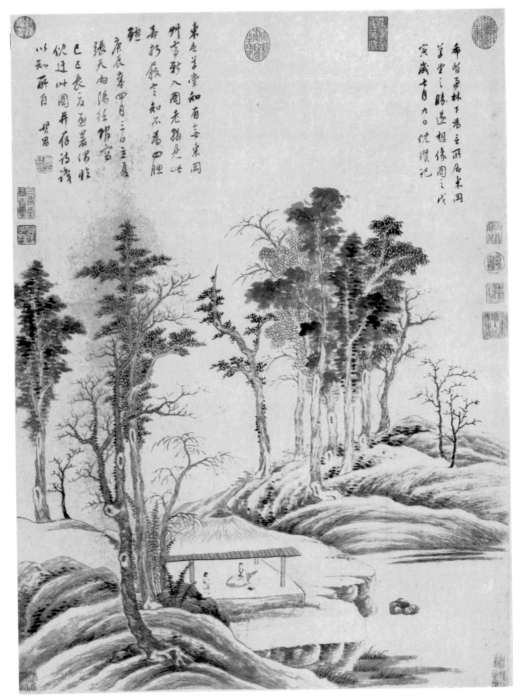

TUNG CH'I-CH'ANG (1555-1636) – THE STRAW HUT ON THE EASTERN HILL – INK ON PAPER (H. 44 3/8". W. 34 3/8")
FORMOSA, NATIONAL GOVERNMENT COLLECTION

art-historical theory which divided all Chinese painters into a Northern and a Southern School—the latter being synonymous with *wên-jên* painting and the only branch of the art worthy of serious consideration. They demanded that a painter should be a disinterested amateur and their theories dominated all art criticism from that time onwards. Tung Ch'i-ch'ang's writings and painting marked a turning point in the art.

Historically speaking, Tung Ch'i-ch'ang belonged to the Wu School which had produced Shên Chou and Wên Ch'êng-ming. But he was a far more gifted and deeper artist than the latter. We can perhaps summarise his art as that of the old masters reinterpreted. Sherman Lee says that he "was both a supreme reactionary and a supreme revolutionist. While the result is a loss of the outward reality, there is a really significant gain in an arbitrary, even fierce, reorganisation of the elements of landscape painting into a monumental format." J.-P. Dubosc, a champion of later painting, praises the fact that his work is "entirely lacking in sweetness and in consequence it is less accessible than the conventional Sung painting, the compositions are free from trivialities and show a classical austerity—one can indeed speak of the noble uniformity of their artistic production." He is in effect a scholar's painter, the polished spokesman of subsequent generations of gentleman painters.

All art, of course, involves selection but those who look for the expression of emotion in one of his paintings will be disappointed. His studies of the old masters led him to a preoccupation with technique, with the possibilities of brush and ink and particularly with the *ts'un* or "wrinkles" which various artists evolved to depict various aspects of landscape such as rocks and clouds. However, he was never simply a copyist for he always stressed the need for an artist to express his own personality through the spirit of the old masters. He personified the Chinese respect for tradition yet at the same time their insistence on new expression so long as it was not too out of context. Many great masters of the past inspired him—especially Tung Yüan but also inter alia, Huang Kung-wang, Wang Mêng, Ni Tsan and Mi Fei, in fact any artist with the right *wên-jên* connections.

Perhaps his most original contribution was in the field of composition. Here he shows a complete freedom in reformulating the visions of earlier masters. They are carefully calculated and highly intellectualised—possibly too much so for many tastes. The painting *The Straw Hut on the Eastern Hill* (Plate 123) is a typical product in a minor key and on the traditional theme of the scholar's hut in a valley. It is dated 1629 and on it he claims that Ni Tsan inspired him. There is in fact very little Ni Tsan left in it—perhaps one or two withered trees, the hut and the flat table of rock on which it sits. The other rocks with their humped contours are more reminiscent of the Five Dynasties in brushwork and have nothing whatsoever to do with Ni Tsan.   Tung Ch'i-ch'ang has replaced the evocative, lonely atmosphere and the pale light of the earlier artist by a lucid, clear-cut crispness.   He is almost mathematical.   He may have seen a Ni Tsan which treats such an intimate segment of nature but generally Ni Tsan painted broad vistas and figures rarely intrude with the calm assumption of authority which we see in Tung Ch'i-ch'ang.   One is tempted to ask how much of the spirit of the ancients really remains in such an interpretation?

Tung Ch'i-ch'ang represents the epitome of Ming art-theory where landscape becomes nothing but an intellectual exercise.   For the full impact of Tung Ch'i-ch'ang's influence and for the revolt it inspired we must turn to the Ch'ing Dynasty.

# The Ch'ing Dynasty
## 1644 - 1911

INTERNAL corruption and external pressure—the constant enemies of all civilisations—brought about the downfall of the Ming Dynasty. During the 16th century warlike nomadic peoples in the north increasingly harrassed the Chinese; repeated Japanese seaborne raids which culminated in a full-scale invasion of Korea, exhausted their resources. Within the country, the palace eunuchs had gained undisputed power and took over the entire administration. They oppressed the provinces in order to enrich themselves, and were able to keep the Emperor in ignorance of the dangerous conditions which their rapacity had created. Officials had to pay these eunuchs highly to secure offices and were then forced to recoup themselves by extortion in the areas which they had "bought". This created widespread unrest, especially in regions farther from the Capital. It led in the 17th century to a rising under a popular leader, Li Tzu-ch'êng who captured Peking in 1644.

Meanwhile, in the first quarter of the 17th century, a capable chieftain had welded the Manchu tribes in the north.

CHU TA (KNOWN AS PA-TA-SHAN-JÊN) — (1626 CIRCA 1705) FISH IN A POND — INK AND SLIGHT COLOUR ON PAPER (H. 47 1/2" W. 13") — OXFORD, AUTHOR'S COLLECTION like the Mongols before them, into a united fighting nation which only a number of able and loyal Chinese generals such as Wu San-kuei, entrenched behind the fortifications of the Great Wall, were able to hold at bay.

When the capital fell to the revolt, the loyal Ming general Wu San-kuei and the rebel leader Li Tzu-ch'êng at first seemed willing to come to terms but then quarrelled bitterly over the possession of a concubine. In pique, Wu invited the Manchus to help him retake Peking and the northern tribes gladly passed through the gates of the Great Wall to occupy the capital. Wu San-kuei pursued his rival to the west, finally defeated him and gained a large southern province as his reward. However, once they had so easily achieved their ambition, there was no question of the Manchus leaving the country.

Thus the Manchus occupied the North on invitation and without protest. But they only conquered the more independent south after decades of bitter warfare. That they were able to achieve this at all was due to the abilities of their second Emperor known by his reign name K'ang-hsi (1662-1722). His two able successors Yung-chêng (1723-1735) and the long-lived Ch'ien-lung (1736-1795) completed his work. They extended the borders of China farther than ever before and gave China a period of economic prosperity such as she had never known. To many of the Christian missionaries who went there, China seemed a greater nation than any in Europe at the time.

The refusal of the south to accept the Manchus further increased the cleavage between it and the north of the country. The class of unemployed, discontented scholars to which we have already referred created a serious political, social and economic problem. The Manchus always mistrusted the rich south and bled it in order to finance grandiose schemes from which the north profited most. Being a foreign and comparatively untutored nation, they always felt somewhat insecure in the face of Chinese culture. They accepted it, but supported only its most orthodox and traditional aspects. This policy won over many scholars and administrators but the most independent spirits were to be found outside the administration and in the cultural centres of the south like Hangchou and Yangchou. It is important in this respect to appreciate that a society with sufficient economic and intellectual backing existed to support a large body of painters. This may have been due in part to the fact that the pattern books created a broad class of amateurs. Many of them were undistinguished but certainly the interest in painting was never so great nor so broadly based.

We have seen how in previous centuries, the scholar-official class produced the painters. Now the two dissimilar arts of painting and politics became peculiarly involved with each other. Scholars outside the administration tended to be iconoclastic and this attitude is reflected in the work of many of the most

127

original thinkers. Until comparatively recently it had been the custom to ignore or denigrate most of the painting of the 17th and 18th centuries but more recently scholars have come to realise that this period is one of the most interesting in the whole history of the art.

We call "individualists" those painters who were responsible for the revolt against Ming scholasticism in the mid 17th century. The three outstanding representatives are Chu Ta, K'un Ts'an and Tao-chi. Between them they completely changed the direction of Chinese painting. A number of early 18th century painters continued their work and many modern Chinese artist owe a great deal to the new styles they evolved.

The peculiar flavour of the works of these individualists is due to a number of features. First, the compositions are completely their own. To this they often add an originality of brushwork which occasionally seems deliberately careless. These two ingredients form the basis of their actual techniques. However, even more important is the new intensity of emotion which we see in their work. The search for new techniques led them sometimes into excesses which are the direct consequences of a determination to escape from the suffocating weight of venerable traditions. However, a new sincerity ensures that their products, even at their most romantic, are never sentimental and weak.

Chu Ta (1626 - ca. 1705) is best known by his other name Pa-ta-shan-jên. He was a member of the Ming Imperial family, passed his examinations for the civil service at a young age, but never actually served. The downfall of the Ming dynasty involved him in its disturbances and dangers and he chose to become a Buddhist monk. Soon afterwards, according to the histories, he went mad, tore his monk's garments and burned them. One day he wrote the character for "dumb" on his door and never again spoke a word to anybody. Many other stories are told of his eccentric behaviour. He seems to have done his best work when he was drunk and gave it away to anybody who happened to be in his company. His personality and way of life come very close to the wild bohemian of European art circles, and indeed with many of the individualists eccentricity became a cult. Chu Ta gained great recognition in his life-time and his paintings were very popular.

He sometimes painted landscapes but most of his work is in the form of albums of birds, fishes and flowers. He gave every subject he touched a personality which immediately distinguishes it. It is impossible to mistake a Pa-ta-shan-jên. An attractive sense of humour pervades much of his work—especially the smaller studies of birds and fish. He seems deliberately to mock the traditional styles and significantly he says that the styles of the Chin and T'ang dynasties inspired his calligraphy. The popular modes of the time meant nothing to him.

128

K'UN TS'AN (KNOWN AS SHI CH'I) –
(BORN CIRCA 1610) – AUTUMN LANDS-
CAPE IN THE RAIN – DATED 1696 –
INK AND COLOUR ON PAPER
(H. 50 1/2″. W. 25″) – OXFORD,
MUSEUM OF EASTERN ART

Plate 126 *Fish in a Pond* is typical of his seemingly careless brushwork and original sense of composition. We seem to be looking down from a bank into the depths of the water where a few fish swim silently with their eyes fixed on the spectator. All his animals seem to have a very definite personality and for the first time in Chinese painting, a human quality. No artist uses space to better advantage and in this he is the true inheritor of the Sung *Ch'an* Buddhist masters. His compositions have a unique simplicity and clarity; the spacing is always the key to the effectiveness of his work. He can make a painting as well from two tiny spiders in the middle of a blank sheet as from a group of birds huddled on a branch. He paints a strange personal world but a touching melancholy lies behind even his most amusing sketches.

The work of the monk K'un Ts'an (also known as Shih Ch'i) illustrates one aspect of the revolt of the 17th century masters against the intellectualism of the late Ming masters and their preoccupation with refined techniques. In K'un Ts'an we see a genuine return to nature, a pure passion for landscape and an overwhelming sincerity of spirit. He was born *ca.* 1610 and most of his known work falls into the period 1660-1674. He, too, found spiritual and possibly political refuge in the Buddhist faith and he rose to be head of a great monastery. Unlike with some of the individualists, Buddhism seems to have been a genuine force in his life. After the fall of the Ming dynasty he became to all intents a hermit and devoted his life to religious meditation and to the administration of his monastery. He seems to have been a man of great moral integrity and religious conviction. He painted purely for his pleasure and his work was comparatively unknown in his own time. His work is perhaps less revolutionary than that of some of his contemporaries but later critics recognised him as one of the really great masters of his and any period.

One late Chinese critic says of his work, "His landscapes represent mysterious scenery, far-reaching, deep and quiet, alluring to the hearts of man. His brushwork was noble and simple, his colours pure and deep as in the great Yüan masters". His large, full-scale compositions do indeed owe much to the Yüan masters. Like them he sees nature as a reality and paints it as a spiritual experience rather than as an exercise. His brushwork owes something to Shên Chou but his interpretations are much more pictorial, warm and emotional. In the soft washes of pink that often cover his paintings, he most successfully fuses landscapes and colour in a manner not achieved by any other painter.

*Autumn Landscape in the Rain* (Plate 129) is dated 1696 and it is probably the latest known picture by him. It was somewhat damaged and has been repaired, in places not very skilfully. Nevertheless about ninety per cent is original. In a calm manner K'un Ts'an has recorded a deep and involved wilderness, taking a humble delight in the complexity of nature. He is so pene-

TAO-CHI (1630-1707) – LANDSCAPE – ALBUM LEAF (H. 8″. W. 10 1/2″) – COLLECTION OF THE LATE K. SUMITOMO, JAPAN

trated by a sense of nature's productive force that he fills his landscapes with detail, not leaving a corner unexplored. Sirén says of his work, "All his art is an endeavour to render in pictorial symbols the creative forces which make nature so overwhelmingly rich, variegated and significant". Where many late Ming painters dissect, K'un Ts'an constructs, lovingly and with a caressing imagination. In this painting a temple nestles in a gully with a path leading up to it. Waterfalls drop from the heights behind. A solitary traveller crosses a bridge at the bottom on his way up to the temple precincts. The inscription, in the mature style of an old man, takes the form of a long poem in praise of the scenery and at the end he says that a brother poet visited him in the rain, took some paper from his sleeve and begged him to paint, whereupon he painted

131

this landscape. One feels the heavy, almost dank wetness of early autumn, an impression heightened by the soft colours. The scenery is highly atmospheric, the mood rich and mellow. K'un Ts'an is without doubt the gentlest of the individualists. There is no protest, conscious or unconscious, in him. He merely looks at the world about him with eyes unclouded by formalism.

The best known of these revolutionary masters is Tao-chi (also known as Shih Tao. The character *shih* means "stone" and it occurs also in of K'un Ts'an's names, Shih Chi. Thus these two artists are often known as "The Two Stones"). Tao-chi lived *ca.* 1630-1714 and painted throughout his long life. He was almost a generation younger than K'un Ts'an. Like Chu Ta, he was of royal Ming descent and he too became a Buddhist monk though his religious duties seem to have rested more lightly on his shoulders than on those of K'un Ts'an. As with many intellectuals and artists, the Buddhist church offered a safe, respected and for many men, a not too demanding alternative to service in the administration. His contemporaries considered him haughty, overbearing and of extremely independent character.

Tao-chi was a man of wide artistic interests—calligrapher, poet, theoretican and landscape gardener. Like most landscape painters of the time he travelled widely but he worked mostly in Yangchou which by this time had become firmly established as one of the period's main centres of cultural activity. Although he left far more paintings than K'un Ts'an, he seems to have prefered to work in small format and produced a number of striking albums. Of all the moden artists he is the most forged. The seeming simplicity of some of his styles lends itself to imitation and there are modern Chinese painters, most competent in their own right, who have specialised in imitating his work.

In his most original writings, Tao-chi made his position quite clear. Although he had due regard for some of the great masters of the past, especially Ni Tsan, he emphasised that copying them had little part in his artistic theory. He claimed that his ambition was "to transform them". His most famous remark illustrates his attitude, "The beards and eyebrows of the old masters cannot grow on my face; the lungs and bowels (the thoughts and feelings) of the old masters cannot be transferred into my stomach (mind)." Living, as we do, in a century when individuality is the touchstone of an artist, it is difficult for us to appreciate just how revolutionary such ideals must have appeared to the Chinese in the 17th century—especially since they came after a period of the most intense appraisal and analysis of the past masters. Although he was a Buddhist, Tao-chi sought sanction for his theories also in ancient *Taoist* metaphysical attitudes "the method which consists in not following any method is the perfect method." He thus claims a complete liberty to develope his own artistic personality.

132

We reproduce here, in plate 131, a leaf from an album of views of Huang-shan. This fantastic mountain formation in Anhui stimulated his imagination and challenged his technical mastery. His view of landscape, as in this water-colour of *A mountain Spring in the Mists of Early Morning*, is highly personal and full of wit. The dignity and austerity of K'un Ts'an have disappeared. The focus of Tao-chi's interest is entirely different from that of this predecessors; more than any other Chinese landscape painter he dominates the natural world he paints, twisting it to suit his mood and sense of humour. His colours are gentle and reasonable, but his brushwork fills even the smallest space with a new power. His observation is less loving than that of K'un Ts'an but he makes a stronger appeal to our emotions and communicates his joy in the natural world with a new spontaneity.

The last 17th century individualist whom we have space to discuss is Kung Hsien (active 1656-1682). His range was more limited than those of the revolutionary painters previously illustrated but, within it, he is perhaps the most impressive and powerful of them all. Considered purely as a landscape painter, he shows the most original imagination and the most forceful style we

KUNG HSIEN (ACTIVE CIRCA 1660-1700) – LANDSCAPE – INK ON PAPER – NEW YORK, WALTER HOCHSTADTER COLLECTION

have yet encountered. It is interesting to note in passing that, although he was not a Buddhist priest, he led a hermit's life and seldom left his home.

The *Landscape* in plate 133 is perhaps his finest surviving work and the most complete expression of his brooding spirit. The westerner will immediately be reminded of landscapes by Altdorfer and even El Greco. Seen in its historical background, it is strange to notice that Kung Hsien seems to go back to the towering mountain formations in the coloured paintings of the T'ang so-called "Northern School" though, of course he interprets them in pure ink tones. Tung Ch'i-ch'ang's disapproval of the Northern masters meant little to him and he rejects completely the rustic idylls of the late Ming—early Ch'ing traditional landscapists whose world was too tame or too artifical to suit his tormented imagination. Kung Hsien's world was not a friendly one; he is trying to return to a primeval landscape in which no human being intrudes. It produces a violent impact. His unique thick wet ink and the striking contrasts of dead white and black create a threatening atmosphere. He spurns the sophisticated and mannered, and brings into Chinese landscape painting the haunted imagination of expressionism. Of his landscape painting he said, "Before me there have been no ancient masters who could do it, after me there will be nobody who can." This was no empty boast.

The individualists did not completely displace the traditional styles. A number of most able artists followed and developed the patterns built up by the *wên-jên* painters in the Ming dynasty. Apologists of the orthodox claim that the finest of these painters were the Six Great Masters of the Ch'ing Dynasty, *i.e.* the Four Wangs, Wu Li and Yün Shou-p'ing. The Four Wangs were Wang Shih-min (1592-1680), Wang Chien (1598-1677), Wang Hui (1632-1717) and Wang Yüan-ch'i (1642-1715). These masters spanned the 17th century and were responsible for the comparatively smooth transition from the Ming to the Ch'ing styles. Fundamentally they continued along paths laid down by Tung Ch'i-ch'ang. Wang Shih-min, the doyen of the group, had studied under Tung Ch'i-ch'ang. Most of these painters had no objection to serving the Manchus as administrators but many retired fairly early in life to devote themselves to the arts.

It is impossible to illustrate the vast field and great variety of even one of these painters. We reproduce in plate 135 a typical landscape by Wang Hui, one of the youngest of the group. He was a man of great natural talent who was fortunate to be accepted by Wang Shih-min as a student. He studied deeply all the great masters of the past—especially the Sung and Yüan masters whom he particularly admired. From each of them he took something. Like many traditional masters of the time he was completely eclectic. The *Landscape*, which is dated 1670 and has an inscription by Wang Shih-min, shows only one

石谷此幅擬山樵而唐六如畫法
發之以石承之宏致風骨萬壑迴
出山橋捃梯之水春曉映地景攬以
見臨谷句數篇之知其巢湖以以
巫遇登兩高峽峽余待谷翁
陟坑晚景月情數其隔滿所在始
如昔人徵斂贼我辰不棄之
庚戍秋仲題二玉峯老人并詩跋題

WANG HUI (1632-1717) — AUTUMN LANDSCAPE —
1670 — INK AND COLOUR ON PAPER — FORMOSA,
NATIONAL GOVERNMENT COLLECTION

of the styles of which he was completely master. He has obviously taken his inspiration from the 14th century painter Wang Mêng. With absolute virtuosity he has created a closely integrated mass of foliage which screens mountains where waterfalls drop and clusters of houses and a temple nestle. The soaring peaks rise nearly to the top of the painting and almost the whole space is covered with accomplished brushwork.

Wherein lies the difference between Wang Hui's painting and that of his inspiration ? First, Wang Hui's work is softer and more atmospheric. His control of depth and distance is far more sophisticated than that of the earlier painter. His use of colour softens the whole scene. Technically the work is far more polished and he is striving for a warm familiarity which the Yüan masters would never have attempted. His preoccupation with dots and lines, which by then were the chief equipment of landscape painters, led him to a degree of urbanity which introduces a charming but false note. It is as if he is trying to outdo the Yüan masters—to produce a vision broader and more complex, but which is at the same time more tame and less sincere. His world is less overpowering and he seems to lose himself within it. In a Yüan painting every brushstroke contributes to its reality, especially in the mountain formations. In Wang Hui whole areas, particularly in his treatment of mountains, express nothing, and his rhythms are not those of nature. It all seems a little too easy and automatic.

Yün Shou-p'ing (1633-1690) was a contemporary and close personal friend of Wang Hui. In his earlier years he painted a number of accomplished landscapes after Yüan masters but he says that the felt Wang Hui was so superior to himself in the art of landscape painting that he abandoned his ambitions in this direction and thenceforth restricted himself to flower painting. This aspect of his work is by far the best known and has received the compliment of frequent imitation in later years. One encounters designs in porcelain and other craftwork which owe much to him. He was particularly skilled in what the Chinese call the « boneless » manner which dispenses with outlines and uses only colour. Plate 139 shows a typical flower painting from the master which obviously goes back to the achievements of the Sung in this type of painting. As a Chinese critic remarked « All the secrets of nature and the joy of such things are gathered at the tip of his brush ». Such flower paintings are the logical conclusion of the Academy painters of the Sung and Ming periods. At the same time it is more than simply a dead botanical study such as many artists of the time produced. He was very conscious of the need for an artist to develop and express his own personality and to capture the ch'i-yün. He combines careful observation, deep knowledge and a sensitive use of colours. Of its kind his work is unsurpassed.

136

The Manchus made sincere efforts to absorb Chinese culture. Vis-à-vis the Chinese they were naturally in a very favoured economic position. Many places in the administration were reserved for them and the competition for position was much less severe among the numerically inferior Manchus than it was between the Chinese. A number of the foreigners became scholars and painters whom even the Chinese respected. Kao Ch'i-p'ei who died in 1734 is perhaps outstanding among them. He rose to high position in the administration and was also a man of artistic ability. He is particularly well-known for his *chih-t'ou-hua* or "finger painting" in which the artist puts the ink and

KAO CH'I-P'EI (XVIIIth CENTURY) – MAN WITH UMBRELLA – FINGER PAINTING – INK AND COLOUR ON PAPER (H. 37″. W. 16″) – LONDON, BRITISH MUSEUM

colour on with his nails or finger tips. From comparatively early times the Chinese had experimented with implements other than the brush and one reads admiring stories of drunken painters who dipped the ends of rope or pieces of rag in the ink and dashed off their masterpieces on the walls of wine-shops. In the Ch'ing dynasty it became fashionable for artists to paint with their fingers. Even the first emperor of the Ch'ing who died in 1661 is said to have been skilled in the technique. One can see in this the desire on the part of some artists not only

HUA YEN (1682-1755) – JACKDAWS – INK ON PAPER (H. 29 1/8,'. W. 20 7/8'')
CHINA, CHANG CHUN COLLECTION

YÜN SHOU-P'ING (1633-1690) – FLOWERS – COLOUR ON
SILK – FORMOSA, NATIONAL GOVERNMENT COLLECTION

to experiment but also to escape from what they felt were the restrictions of
painting with a brush—techniques which by this time had been so thoroughly
explored.   It is in effect another aspect of the revolt against the pattern books.

Kao Ch'i-p'ei is acknowledged to be the outstanding artist of *chih-t'ou-
hua*.   Plate 137 *Man with Umbrella* is characteristic of his work.   It gives the
impression of a mastered virtuosity and an unforced originality.   The seemingly
careless technique and the rapidity of execution conceal a remarkably accom-

plished draughtsmanship. One sees in his use of ink and his understanding of
the value of space another attempt to revive *Ch'an* painting ideals but here
without the religious content. In a sense the abandonment of the brush was
the logical conclusion to the splashed ink technique of Sung times. Having
abandoned line, artists probably felt that they could dispense with the brush
on which it depended. Their humour shows them trying to escape from the
self-conscious seriousness of the Ming scholars.

An important indication of the fresh winds blowing through the ancient
art of painting in the 17th and 18th centuries is the fact that many of the most
famous artists did not study under any particular master. Their biographies
often do not state than they even *studied* the works of earlier painters. For an
art so conscious of past achievements, this is in itself revolutionary. Often these
painters seem to pride themselves on not owing anything whatsoever to the past.

Many of them lived either in Hangchou or in Yangchou. The latter, a
beautiful riverside city, contained a large proportion of the free-thinking men
of the time. The history of this city and its influence on the intellectual life of
the period would make a fascinating story. Here lived the wealthy patrons
of the arts—men who had grown rich from enterprises like the salt monopoly.
They built great libraries and acted as generous hosts to the many poor and
unemployed scholars who gathered there from all over China. One reads of
the parties they gave in their famous gardens and of the researches they subsi-
dised. In all studies the spirit of iconoclasm ran high—scholars bitterly attacked

140

the interpretation of Confucianism which Chu Hsi made official in the 12th century and sought their authority in ancient and purer texts of the classics. For a while the scholars were outspoken but later, in the 18th century they were forced to be more guarded.   The Manchu rulers, especially Ch'ien-lung, initiated literary inquisitions which, under the guise of scholarship, aimed at rooting out all revolutionary ideas which might be construed as dangerous to the established regime.   However, it must be admitted that the scholars' opposition was sometimes little more than intellectual nostalgia or pique at not finding the place within the administration which their abilities merited.

Hua Yen (1682-1755) was one of the many artists whom Yangchou attracted.   His *Jackdaws* in plate 138 shows him in a free yet sensitive mood. His work here certainly owes something to Chu Ta.   He has infused the two birds huddled on a branch in the cold with an intense brooding atmosphere. With a few telling brushstrokes he has created all the bleakness of winter. Hua Yen sometimes painted strange intimate landscapes while at other times, in a twig of plum blossom or in a bird he seeks new forms of expression which try deliberately to break with the past.   Nevertheless he could not break entirely with his tradition.   It is interesting to compare his work with that of Emperor Hui-tsung in plate 73.   Hua Yen seems to be trying to revive and reinterpret the old academic style.   However, like many artists of the period he was completely eclectic and the only common denominator in the work of them all is a weariness with the old styles of *wên-jên* painting.   The Chinese say of his work

"The meaning behind his brush was loose and relaxed" and they add, "He did not seek the elegant and coquetish".

During the first century of the Ch'ing dynasty, until about 1760, so many very able painters flourished, and among them one sees such a diversity of styles that Chinese historians quite understandably lose their way in trying to classify them into the neat schools and genealogies which are so dear to them. The best they can do is to group the various artists under names of towns or areas in which they lived. Stylistically these group names mean little—at most they indicate a common intellectual background and similar interests.

The most significant of these groups is "The Eight Eccentrics (or Strange Masters) of Yangchou". Some historians include Hua Yen in the group but in reality he does not belong to it. The works of this interesting group have had the greatest influence on subsequent Chinese painting down to the present day and were of particular importance to Japanese ink painting. Its leader was Chin Nung (1687-1764) who started his artistic career as a calligrapher and was the most deliberately revolutionary of them all. It cannot be stressed too strongly that the clue to the understanding of much early Ch'ing painting lies

LI SHAN (FIRST HALF OF THE XVIIIth CENTURY) – BAMBOO IN THE MIST – ALBUM LEAF – INK ON PAPER (H. 8 1/8". W. 13 5/8")
OXFORD, AUTHOR'S COLLECTION

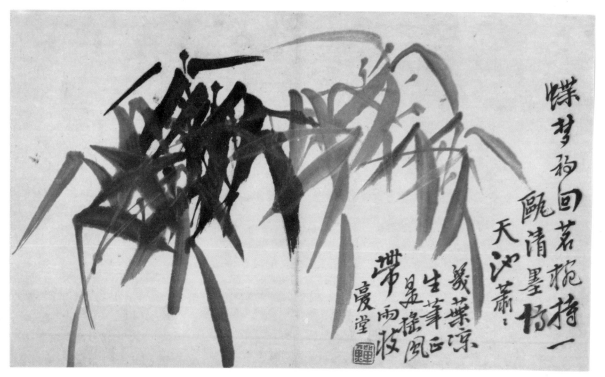

CHANG SHIH-PAO (LATE XIXth CEN-
TURY) – THE GOD OF LONGEVITY –
INK AND SLIGHT COLOUR ON
PAPER (H. 52 1/2″. W. 25″) –
OXFORD, AUTHOR'S COLLECTION

in an appreciation of their calligraphy. This should not deter the westerner without any understanding or experience in calligraphy for one can immediately see, for example, in Chin Nung's powerful, carving-like writing executed with a worn brush, an individual style which appears here for the first time. He deliberately makes his strokes the antithesis of the fluid, elegant brushwork of the traditional styles. He started to paint comparatively late in life, in his late forties, possibly led to do so by the success of his calligraphy. He openly spurned most of the Sung and Ming masters and professed to return to T'ang and pre-T'ang ideals. He had probably seen few original works of these early periods and his attachment to them was most likely a purely literary affectation. In effect, it gave him the freedom, backed by an imaginary authority, to explore whatever forms he liked. Many of his paintings are eccentric in the extreme. However, it is significant that he could not take the final step and cut himself off from reliance on all authority and tradition. This was what Chinese painting needed to bring about a complete revival.

During this period the *wên-jên* ideals completely broke down. Chin Nung was certainly a scholar painter imbued with the ideal that a painter should be an amateur and above all financial considerations. But, as a result of the economic conditions described above, he was forced openly to live by his artistic skill. He was prepared to sell or barter his painting for food and money and occasionally he records how he was "deeply ashamed in comparison with the black-robed classes (the Buddhist monks)". He admired the monks and lived in the atmosphere of the temples but he never actually entered the church.

Plate 140, one of his last paintings, done at the age of seventy-six, shows no diminution of his powers. The subjects is a traditional one but he has treated it in a vigorous manner which is completely new. The combination of calligraphy and painting produces a masterly effect of a cold day of late winter when the early-flowering plum blossoms give hope of spring. It was done, as he says in the inscription before "the spring had leaked out". Here his calligraphy and painting match each other in their obstinate strength. In other equally individual works he tried to revive elements of the Buddhist painting of T'ang and Sung times.

The last of the Yangchou individualists we can here illustrate is Li Shan who was slightly younger than Chin Nung. He served the administration but is said to have offended a superior, was relieved of his post and returned home to live henceforth independently as a painter. Comparison with Plate 121 will immediately show how Hsü Wei influenced him and it is possible to see influences also from such artists as Kao Ch'i-p'ei. Chinese critics are divided on the quality of his work, some deride his "bustling brushwork", others praise his ability to penetrate the spirit of nature. Plate 142, *Bamboos in the Mist* is taken from an

144

album of Flowers, Insects and Birds. Here is another very individual style of calligraphy which seems to dance over the paper. The most striking aspect of his work is his unique ink tones. He seems to have applied the ink on the paper while it was wet, thus softening it and giving it added nuances. The technique gives some of his paintings a luminous quality and imparts a new and delicate sense of light on surfaces. On another page of the same album he says that he is concerned with expressing the *ta-i* "the great meaning", the fundamental spirit of his subject. Like many of these painters he genuinely seeks to see things in a fresh way. He is a far more sophisticated painter than Chin Nung who perhaps was too revolutionary for most of his contemporaries apart from his immediate pupils. Li Shan provided just that degree of combined originality and skill which his contemporaries could accept, and by traditional Chinese standards he is perhaps the finest painter among the Eight Eccentrics. His style has greatly influenced many modern Chinese artists.

The demand for originality, as we have seen in the west during this century, can be the greatest tyranny to afflict an artist. It led some of the Chinese individualists into an attitude of "nothing succeeds like excess". It is interesting to speculate why they could not entirely shake off the weight of their own tradition, for their inability to do so restricted the future of Chinese painting. It may well have been that the respect for nature was so deeply rooted in the Chinese mentality that they were unwilling to go beyond a certain point in their liberties with it.

The innovations of the early 18th century masters lasted until the present time with steadily decreasing power. However, it is a mistake to ignore completely the work of all the 19th century masters indiscriminately. Although the tide of creation was waning, some artists were worthy inheritors of the centuries old Chinese skill with the brush. We illustrate here a painting by the 19th century painter Chang Shih-pao which is dated 1871. It is of *Shou-Lao*, the God of Longevity. He is often shown, as here, as a white haired old man carrying a peach which is said to come from a fabulous tree which blossoms only once in every three thousand years and yields its fruit three thousand years after that. From his pocket hangs a piece of *ling-chih* fungus which also is supposed to give immortality (Plate 143), Chang Shih-pao combines the ink tones of Li Shan with the figure painting of another of the Eight Eccentrics, Huang Shên. The Chinese praise his air of "antique refinement". The brushwork is excellent, the characterisation leaves nothing to be desired. It is the work of the individualists digested and rendered in the more traditional and to most Chinese, more acceptable terms.

WE have now surveyed, however briefly, more than two thousand years of Chinese painting. The reader will be tempted to ask, what of the present and future of the art? The Chinese in this century have produced a few artists who have gained international reputation,—Ch'i Pai-shih and Ju Peon are both first class technicians and colourists. Their art springs from the innovators of the 18th century such as Li Shan but, in common with most modern Chinese painters, they use a more colourful palette.

With the 19th century military and political supremacy of the west, many Chinese artists, like their colleagues in Japan, turned to European art forms and techniques. For example, oil painting became very popular and even now the Chinese produce essays in social realism which are only too frankly 19th century in approach and execution.

Real Chinese painting is sufficiently flexible still to offer a great deal to the world of painting. Perhaps it will broaden its outlook, for in the modern world art has become internationalised. The discoveries of western painters belong as much to the Chinese as they do to the west. With the recovery of their independence and their pride, Chinese artists may well have something to offer the west. Recently some relatively obscure Chinese artists, most of them however living outside their homeland, have shown how, without any sacrifice of their traditions, they can make a valid synthesis of east and west. If the authorities do not forbid such art as "decadent" and "capitalist", there is no reason why in China proper, we should not see a revival of the art. The Japanese are steadily working towards such a new far-eastern painting.

As a conclusion to this short work, the author would like to emphasize that the study and appreciation of Chinese painting does not belong exclusively to the expert. Specialist knowledge can, to a degree, heighten our appreciation, but improperly used it can equally cloud the vision. The study of Chinese painting can be just as rewarding to the amateur who is prepared to give himself to it with the same enthusiasm as he would to western painting. If he is ready to develop a critical faculty and is not awed or put off by the unfamiliar he will find that all artists are alike under the skin and that the language of painting is universal.

147

檣船
宜於月下及霞靄中
使人見之如聞欸刀

1 – *Chinese Landscape Painting*, Cleveland, U.S.A., 1954.

2 – Arthur WALEY, *The Book of Songs*, London, 1937, p. 120.

3 – *Chiu Chang, She Chiang*, 3rd century B.C., Trans. David HAWKES.

4 – C. P. FITZGERALD, *China*, London, 1935, p. 270.

5 – Chinese Commentaries on these succinctly stated principles are almost matched by the efforts of western scholars to translate and interpret them. The version given is by W. ACKER which he arrived at after the most detailed study.

6 – *Chinese Art*, London, 1935.

7 – *China*, London 1935, p. 399.

8 – From the *Saddharma-Pundarika Sutra*, translated by Richard ROBINSON, in *Chinese Buddhist Verse*; London, 1954.

9 – *The Art and Architecture of China*, London, 1956.

10 – Translated by Wm. A. ROULSTON, *Oriental Art*, Vol. II, n° 4.

11 – W. COHN, *Chinese Painting*, London 1948.

12 – *An Essay on Landscape Painting*, translated by S. SAKANISHI, London, 1935.

13 – Translations by S. JENYNS.

14 – Derke BODDE, in *China*, U.S.A., 1946.

15 – *Op. cit.*, translated by S. SAKANISHI.

16 – S. SAKANISHI. *The Spirit of the Brush*, London, 1939.

17 – Trans. CHING TI, in *The White Pony*, London, 1949.

18 – *The Gay Genius*, London and New York, 1947.

19 – Translated by Arthur WALEY under the title *Monkey*, London, 1942.

20 – A. K. COOMARASWAMY, *The Transformation of Nature in Art*, New York 1956 (reprint).

21 – Y. YONEZAWA and S. SHIMADA, *Painting of the Sung and Yüan Dynasties*, Tokio, 1952.

22 – R. GROUSSET, *La Chine*, in *Les Civilisations de l'Orient*, Paris, 1930.

23 – L. SICKMAN, *The Art and Architecture of China*, London, 1956, p. 140.

24 – SIRÉN, *op. cit.*

25 – SIRÉN, *op. cit.*

26 – T. VOLKER, *The Animal in Far Eastern Art*, Leiden, 1950.

27 – KUO HSI.

28 – The best-known of these pattern-books was recently published in English: *The Tao of Painting (A Study of the Ritual Disposition of Chinese Painting)*, with translation of the *Chieh Tzŭ Yüan Hua Chuan*, or *Mustard Seed garden Manual of Painting*, 1679-1701, by MAI-MAI SZE, Routledge and Kegan Paul, Ltd., London, 1957. — 2 vol. Bk.I : 164 pages, 10 plates including 2 coloured plates; Bk.II : 588 pages with 424 reproductions of samples.

We have selected a few characteristic designs. They are here reproduced as vignettes in the text.

Front end-papers - Bamboos.

P. 12 – " Method of painting a stream debouching from the mountains." *(The Book of Rocks.)*

P. 60 – " When Ma Yüan painted pine-trees they were often lean and strong like bent iron. " *(The Book of Trees).*

P. 102 – " Example of leaves hanging downwards. " *(The Book of Orchids.)*

P. 125 – " Another method of making a main peak twisting round on itself. " *(The Book of Rocks.)*

P. 148 – " Rowing boats amidst the reeds under the moonlight. To see them is to hear the paddling of the oars." *(The Book of Jên-wu.)*

End-papers - Orchid Plant. *(The Book of Orchids.)*

29 – SIRÉN, *op. cit.*, II, p. 14.

30 – O. SIRÉN, *The Chinese on the Art of Painting*, Peking, 1936.

# BIBLIOGRAPHY

It would not be difficult to compile a long bibliography on Chinese painting but most of the works listed in it would be almost impossible for the general reader to obtain. Many of them would be in eastern languages and the rest were published in limited editions which are long out of print. The short list below will therefore contain only a few basic books which can be either purchased now or consulted in any reasonably comprehensive library. The longer bibliographies in these specialist studies will, in their turn, take the reader further should he wish to pursue the subject. Most European countries contain at least one specialist library which should satisfy the most enthusiastic amateur. In Paris, the Musée Guimet, in London the British Museum contain splendid libraries.

1 – O. SIRÉN, *A History of Early Chinese Painting*, 2 vols. London, 1927-8.
   *A History of Later Chinese Painting*, 2 vols. London, 1938.
   These volumes are now in course of extensive revision and rewriting. Three volumes have already appeared *Chinese Painting*, London, 1957, and another four, to complete the new set, will appear in 1958.
2 – L. SICKMANN and A. SOPER, *The Art and Architecture of China*, London, 1956.
3 – W. COHN, *Chinese Painting*, London, 1948.
4 – A. WALEY, *An Introduction to the Study of Chinese Painting*, London, 1923.
5 – W. L. BINYON, *Painting in the Far East*, London, 1934.

# COLLECTIONS

The finest public collections of Chinese painting in the West are in the museums of the United States, particularly in the Museum of Fine Arts, Boston; the Freer Gallery, Washington; the William Rockhill Nelson Gallery, Kansas City; the Metropolitan Museum, New York; the Art Institute, Chicago. In Europe, the British Museum, the Musée Guimet and the Musée Cernuschi and the National Museum, Stockholm contain the best collections.

In the Far East the finest collection, that of the ex-Imperial Household, is now housed in Formosa and the authorities of the National Museum there are making great efforts to make it available to the public in reproduction. On the mainland, museums like the Shanghai City Museum are building up impressive collections. Japan is extremely rich in good collections and these are centred in such institutions as the National Museum, Tokyo; the National Museum, Kyoto; the Nezu Museum, Tokyo; the Osaka City Museum, etc.

All the above provide *comparatively* easy conditions for study. However, the very nature of Chinese paintings makes their inspection a matter for great care and special conditions. The student who wishes to pursue further this absorbing subject will require some experience and often introductions—especially in the far east—but his patience and study will be well rewarded.

# LIST OF PLATES

151

152

# TABLE OF CONTENTS

ND 1040 .S92 1967

Swann, Peter C.

Chinese painting

DATE                    ISSUED TO

ND 1040 .S92 1967

Swann, Peter C.

Chinese painting

DEMCO